FACE TO FACE

Praying
the Scriptures
for
Intimate
Worship

Scripture translation and adaptation by

KENNETH BOA

ZondervanPublishingHouse
Grand Rapids, Michigan

A Division of HarperCollins*Publishers*

Face to Face: Praying the Scriptures for Intimate Worship
Copyright © 1997 by Kenneth Boa

Published by:
ZondervanPublishingHouse
Grand Rapids, Michigan 49530
http://www.zondervan.com

Library of Congress Catalog Card Number 97-060198

This edition printed on acid-free paper and meets the American National
Standards Institute Z39.48 standard.

Printed in the United States of America

06 /❖ DC/ 31 30 29 28 27 26

CONTENTS

DEDICATION

To my bride Karen

My beloved companion, colaborer
and fellow sojourner
in our spiritual journey
to the celestial city of God.

INTRODUCTION

The Purpose of This Book

Spiritual growth is impossible apart from the practice of prayer. Just as the key to quality relationships with other people is time spent in communication, so the key to a growing relationship with the personal God of heaven and earth is time invested in speaking to Him in prayer and listening to His voice in Scripture.

As central as these twin disciplines of prayer and Scripture are to our spiritual life, most believers in Jesus Christ are frustrated by hit-or-miss approaches to both. As a result, their time in prayer and the Word can become unsatisfying, routine and even boring. It is no surprise, then, that most people spend a minimal amount of time in either of these disciplines and fail to develop intimacy with the One for whom they were created.

The problem with prayer is heightened by the fact that people often succumb either to the extreme of all form and no freedom, or the opposite extreme of all freedom and no form. The first extreme leads to a rote or impersonal approach to prayer, while the second produces an unbalanced and undisciplined prayer life that can degenerate into a litany of one "gimme" after another. *Face to Face: Praying the Scriptures for Intimate Worship* was designed to make prayer a more enriching and satisfying experience by providing both form and freedom in the practice of prayer.

The Structure of This Book

Think of this book as a tool that combines the word of the Lord with prayer and guides you through the process of praying Scripture back to God. It will enable you to think God's thoughts after Him and to personalize them in your own thinking and practice. It will also provide you with a balanced prayer experience by guiding you each day through eight kinds of prayer. Because it is based on Scripture, you can be assured that these prayers will be pleasing to God. This book will encourage you in your walk with God by enriching and enhancing the quality of your experience of prayer.

Years ago, Max Anders and I were profoundly influenced by the *Private Devotions* of Lancelot Andrewes, a seventeenth-century Anglican bishop and prominent translator of the King James Bible. Andrewes adapted Scripture into various forms of prayer, and this idea prompted us to create a tool for personal and group prayer. *Face to Face: Praying the Scriptures for Intimate Worship* utilizes a section entitled Morning Affirmations as well as a three-month Daily Prayer Guide.

To create this collection of Biblical prayers, I consulted several translations as well as the original language of every passage. The result is essentially my own translation, though it shares much in common with existing translations. My intention in doing this was to remain as close to the Biblical text as possible while still retaining clarity and readability. I then adapted the passages into a personalized format so that they could be used readily in the context of individual and group prayer.

This book of Scriptural prayers is structured around eight forms of prayer which are based on the model of The Lord's Prayer. Our Lord told His disciples to pray in this way:

Father in heaven,
Hallowed be Your name.
Your kingdom come;
Your will be done
On earth as it is in heaven.
Give us today our daily bread,

And forgive us our debts as we also have forgiven our
    debtors.
And lead us not into temptation,
But deliver us from the evil one.
For Yours is the kingdom and the power and the glory
    forever. (Matthew 6:9–13)

The eight forms of adoration, confession, renewal, petition, intercession, affirmation, thanksgiving and closing
prayer are all illustrated in this model prayer:

"Father in heaven, hallowed be Your name"—The
prayer principles of *adoration* (praise for who God is)
and *thanksgiving* (praise for what He has done).

"Your kingdom come; Your will be done on earth as it
is in heaven"—The principle of *affirmation*, that is,
agreeing with God's will and submitting to it.

"Give us our daily bread"—The principle of supplication, in which we make requests both for ourselves
(*petition*) and for others (*intercession*).

"And forgive us our debts as we also have forgiven our
debtors"—The principle of *confession* in view of our
need for forgiveness of sins.

"And lead us not into temptation, but deliver us from
the evil one"—The necessity of *renewal* as we face the
temptations of the world, the flesh and the devil.

"For Yours is the kingdom and the power and the glory
forever"—A *closing prayer* that honors the Lord and
completes our thoughts.

The prayers of petition are formatted around a seven-day
cycle: growth in Christ, growth in wisdom, spiritual insight,
relationships with others, faithfulness as a steward, family
and ministry, and personal concerns.

The prayers of intercession are also based on a weekly cycle: churches and ministries, family, believers, evangelism, government, missions and world affairs.

How To Use This Book

Face to Face: Praying the Scriptures for Intimate Worship consists of three parts: Morning Affirmations, a Daily Prayer Guide and Personal Prayer Pages.

Part One: Morning Affirmations

This set of affirmations is a tool designed to help you renew your mind at the beginning of each day. It can be used by itself or in conjunction with the Daily Prayer Guide as time allows. Morning Affirmations guides you through a Biblical perspective on the fundamental issues of life: *Who am I? Where did I come from? Why am I here? Where am I going?* In this way, you review God's perspective on your faith, your identity, your purpose and your hope.

You needn't feel compelled to go through all the passages in Morning Affirmations every time. As the content becomes more familiar, avoid the trap of reducing these affirmations to a set of words you repeat by rote. Use them as a preliminary to prayer and Bible reading, not as a substitute.

Part Two: Daily Prayer Guide

This is the heart of this book. Because these prayers are on a three-month cycle, you will encounter each passage only four times a year. Thus, this guide can be used indefinitely without excessive repetition.

Be sure to use the prayer prompts so that you do not merely read the prayers. It is essential that you personalize them so that they can be incorporated in your own thoughts and experience.

You can adapt the prayers in each day to differing time formats. They can be used with profit in a short period of time, or you can move through them more slowly, as you see fit.

Although you can tie these daily prayers to the day of the month, there is no need to do so, particularly if you find yourself falling behind. You may decide to mark your place and continue wherever you left off.

Part Three: Personal Prayer Pages

I encourage you to use these pages to add your own thoughts and prayers as they come to mind when using this book. You can also use this section to record your petitionary and intercessory prayers as well as specific answers to prayer.

The Philosophy Underlying This Book

The God of the Bible is infinite, personal and triune. As a communion of three Persons, one of God's purposes in creating us is to display the glory of His being and attributes to intelligent moral creatures who are capable of responding to His relational initiatives. In spite of human rebellion and sin against the Person and character of the Lord, Jesus Christ bore the awesome price of our guilt and inaugurated "a new and living way" (Hebrews 10:20 NIV) by which the barrier to personal relationship with God has been overcome. "This is how God showed his love among us: He sent his one and only Son into the world that we might live through him. This is love: not that we loved God, but that he loved us and sent his Son as an atoning sacrifice for our sins" (1 John 4:9–10 NIV).

Because God is the initiator of a loving relationship with us, our high and holy calling is to respond to His offer. Our Lord, in encapsulating the Law and the Prophets, gave us the essence of this response: "Jesus replied: 'Love the Lord your God with all your heart and with all your soul and with all your mind.' This is the first and greatest commandment. And the second is like it: 'Love your neighbor as yourself.'"

(Matthew 22:37–39 NIV). The quality of our vertical relationship with God has a direct bearing on the quality of our horizontal relationships with others. As we grow in His grace, we will have an enhanced capacity, through the power of the indwelling Holy Spirit, to respond to others with Christlike qualities, being "completely humble, gentle and patient, bearing with one another in love" (Ephesians 4:2 NIV). This *agape* love, which we receive from the Lord and which flows through us toward others, is rooted in volition (our willingness to receive and display it) and is expressed in deeds of other-centered love.

Another way of summarizing our calling and purpose as followers of Jesus is to love God completely, to love self correctly and to love others compassionately.

Loving God completely is a growth process that involves the personal elements of communication and response. By listening to the Holy Spirit in the words of Scripture and speaking to the Lord in our thoughts and prayers, we move in the direction of knowing Him better. The better we know Him, the more we will love Him, and the more we love Him, the greater will be our willingness to respond to Him in trust and obedience.

To *love ourselves correctly* is to see ourselves as God sees us and to allow the Word, not the world, to define who and whose we really are. The clearer we capture the vision of our new identity in Jesus Christ, the more we will realize that our deepest needs for security, significance, and satisfaction are met in Him and not in people, possessions or positions.

A Biblical view of our identity and resources in Christ moves us in the direction of *loving others compassionately*. Grasping our true and unlimited resources in Christ frees us from bondage to the opinions of others and gives us the liberty to love and serve others regardless of their response.

Because we cannot serve two masters, the focus of our heart will either be the temporal or the eternal. If it is the temporal, we cannot love God completely because we will have a divided heart. When Jesus Christ is a single component instead of the center of life, things become complicated; the worries of the world, the deceitfulness of wealth and the desires for other things choke the word of truth in our lives, and we do not bear lasting fruit (Mark 4:19). If the focus of our heart is the eternal, we will love Jesus Christ above His created goods and pleasures and begin to fulfill the enduring purpose for which we were created.

PART ONE

Morning Affirmations

Submitting to God

I submit myself and my life to you, O God:

In view of Your mercy, O God, may I present my body as a
living sacrifice, holy and pleasing to You, which is my reasonable service. May I not be conformed to the pattern of
this world but be transformed by the renewing of my mind,
that I may prove that Your will is good and acceptable and
perfect. (Romans 12:1–2)

Adoration and Thanksgiving

*For who You are and what you have done, accept my praise, O
Lord:*

I will exalt You, my God and King;
I will bless Your name for ever and ever.
Every day I will bless You,
And I will praise Your name for ever and ever.
Great are You, Lord, and most worthy of praise;
Your greatness is unsearchable.
One generation shall praise Your works to another
And shall declare Your mighty acts.
I will meditate on the glorious splendor of Your majesty
And on Your wonderful works.
Many shall speak of the might of Your awesome works,
And I will proclaim Your great deeds.
I will express the memory of Your abundant goodness
And joyfully sing of Your righteousness.
You, O Lord, are gracious and compassionate,
Slow to anger, and great in lovingkindness.
You are good to all,
And Your tender mercies are over all Your works.
    (Psalm 145:1–9)

For who You are and for what You have done, accept my thanks, O Lord:

> Blessed are You, O Lord,
> For You have heard the voice of my prayers.
> You are my strength and my shield;
> My heart trusts in You, and I am helped.
> My heart greatly rejoices,
> And I will give thanks to You in song. (Psalm 28:6–7)

Examination

Holy Spirit, search my heart and reveal to me any unconfessed sin you find in me:

> Search me, O God, and know my heart;
> Test me and know my anxious thoughts.
> See if there is any offensive way in me,
> And lead me in the way everlasting. (Psalm 139:23–24)

Lord, I thank you for the forgiveness you promised when you said:

> "Come now, let us reason together:
> Though your sins are like scarlet,
> They shall be as white as snow;
> Though they are red as crimson,
> They shall be like wool." (Isaiah 1:18)

My Identity in Christ

I rejoice, Lord Jesus, in the identity I have in You:

I have been crucified with You and it is no longer I who live, but You who live in me; and the life which I now live in the flesh I live by faith in You, the Son of God, who loved me, and delivered Yourself up for me. (Galatians 2:20)

I have forgiveness from the penalty of sin because You died for me:

But You, O God, demonstrate Your own love for us in that, while we were still sinners, Christ died for us. (Romans 5:8)

I have freedom from the power of sin because I died with You:

In You, O Christ, I was circumcised with a circumcision made without hands, in the removal of the body of the flesh by Your circumcision, having been buried with You in baptism and raised with You through faith in the working of God, who raised You from the dead. (Colossians 2:11–12)

I have fulfillment for this day because You live in me:

I eagerly expect and hope that I will in no way be ashamed, but will have sufficient courage so that now as always You, Jesus Christ, will be exalted in my body, whether by life or by death. For to me, to live in You, Jesus Christ, means everything and to die is gain. (Philippians 1:20–21)

By faith, I will allow You, O Christ, to manifest Your life through me:

Thanks be to God, who always leads us in triumph in You and through us spreads everywhere the fragrance of the knowledge of You. (2 Corinthians 2:14)

Filling of the Spirit

Holy Spirit, control me and fill me today:

I was once darkness, but now I am light in You, O Lord. May I walk as a child of light (for the fruit of the light consists in all goodness and righteousness and truth), learning what is pleasing to You. (Ephesians 5:18)

As I walk in You, O Spirit, I will not fulfill the desires of the flesh. For the flesh desires what is contrary to You, and You,

Holy Spirit, desire what is contrary to the flesh; for you oppose each other, so that I may not do the things that I wish. But if I am led by You, I am not under the law. (Galatians 5:16)

Since I live in You, Spirit, may I also walk in You. (Galatians 5:25)

Fruit of the Spirit
Holy Spirit, may your fruit grow in me:

But Your fruit, O Holy Spirit, is love, joy, peace, patience, kindness, goodness, faithfulness, gentleness and self-control; against such things there is no law. (Galatians 5:19–23)

I want to glorify the Father by bearing much fruit and so prove to be Christ's disciple. (John 15:8)

Purpose of My Life
O Lord, may your purpose be fulfilled in my life today—to love You completely, to love myself correctly and to love others compassionately:

I will seek first Your kingdom and Your righteousness. (Matthew 6:33)

I want to love You, O Lord my God, with all my heart, and with all my soul, and with all my mind, and I want to love my neighbor as myself. (Matthew 22:37, 39)

Lord, the love we have from You is patient, it is kind, it does not envy; love does not boast, it is not arrogant, it does not behave rudely; it does not seek its own, it is not easily provoked, it keeps no record of wrongs; it does not rejoice in unrighteousness, but rejoices with the truth; it bears all things, believes all things, hopes all things, endures all things. Love never fails. (1 Corinthians 13:4–7)

I will be a witness to those who do not know You, Jesus, and I will participate in Your Great Commission:

I have been called to follow You, Jesus Christ, and to be a fisher of people. (Matthew 4:19)

You have called us to go and make disciples of all nations and You are with us always. (Matthew 28:19–20)

We will be Your witnesses to the ends of the earth. (Acts 1:8)

Circumstances of the Day

I commit my day to You, O Lord:

O God, I know that all things work together for good to those who love you, to those who have been called according to Your purpose. Those you foreknew, You also predestined to be conformed to the likeness of Your Son, that You might be the firstborn among many brothers and sisters. (Romans 8:28–29)

I will obey You today and trust You for all my needs:

I will trust in You, Lord, with all my heart, and not lean on my own understanding. In all my ways I will acknowledge You, and You will make my paths straight. (Proverbs 3:5–6)

Protection in Spiritual Warfare

O Lord, guard my heart against the temptations of the world and renew my heart and spirit:

Since I have been raised up with You, O Christ, I will keep seeking the things above, where You are at the right hand of God. I will set my mind on the things above, not on the things that are on earth. (Colossians 3:1–2)

I will be anxious for nothing, but in everything by prayer and supplication with thanksgiving I will let my requests be made known to You, O God. And Your peace, which surpasses all comprehension, shall guard my heart and my mind in Christ Jesus. (Philippians 4:6–8)

Whatever is true, whatever is honorable, whatever is right, whatever is pure, whatever is lovely, whatever is of good repute, if there is any excellence and anything worthy of praise, I will let my mind dwell on these things. (Philippians 4:9).

O Lord, guard my heart against the weaknesses and temptation of the flesh so that I may reckon myself dead to sin:

Father, I know that my old self was crucified with Christ, so that I am no longer a slave to sin, for he who has died is freed from sin. I will reckon myself as dead to sin, but alive to You in Christ Jesus. I will not present the parts of my body to sin as instruments of unrighteousness, but I will present myself to You, O God, as one alive from the dead, and the parts of my body as instruments of righteousness to You. (Romans 6:6–7, 12–13)

O Lord, guard my heart against the attacks of the devil and give me the strength to resist him:

As I submit myself to You, O God, and resist the devil, he will flee from me. (James 4:7)

I will be of sober spirit and on the alert. My adversary, the devil, prowls about like a roaring lion, seeking someone to devour. But I will resist him, firm in my faith. (1 Peter 5:8–9)

I will take up Your full armor, O God, that I may be able to resist and stand firm. I put on the belt of truth and the breastplate of righteousness; I put on my feet the preparation of the gospel of peace; and I take up the shield of faith with which I will be able to extinguish all the flaming missiles of the evil one. I take the helmet of salvation and the sword of Your Spirit, which is Your Word, O God. With all prayer and petition I will pray at all times in Your Spirit and be on the alert with all perseverance and petition for all the saints. (Ephesians 6:13–18)

The Coming of Christ and My Future With Him

Lord Jesus, I eagerly await the day when You will come again:

Your kingdom come, Your will be done. (Matthew 6:10)

You have said, "I am coming quickly." Amen. Come, Lord Jesus. (Revelation 22:20)

I consider that the sufferings of this present time are not worthy to be compared with the glory that is to be revealed to me. (Romans 8:18)

I will not lose heart, but though my outer self is decaying, yet my inner self is being renewed day by day. For momentary, light affliction is producing for me an eternal weight of glory far beyond all comparison, while I look not at the things which are seen, but at the things which are not seen; for the things which are seen are temporal, but the things which are not seen are eternal. (2 Corinthians 4:16–18)

My citizenship is in heaven, from which also I eagerly wait for You, my Savior, my Lord Jesus Christ. (Philippians 3:20)

PART TWO

Daily Prayer Guide

THE FIRST MONTH

DAY 1

Adoration

O Lord, our Lord,
How majestic is Your name in all the earth!
You have set Your glory above the heavens! (Psalm 8:1)

Great and marvelous are Your works,
Lord God Almighty!
Righteous and true are Your ways,
King of the nations!
Who will not fear You, O Lord, and glorify Your name?
For You alone are holy.
All nations will come and worship before You,
For Your righteous acts have been revealed.
(Revelation 15:3–4)

Pause to express your thoughts of praise and worship.

Confession

You, Lord, are in Your holy temple;
You are on Your heavenly throne.
You observe all people;
Your eyes examine them. (Psalm 11:4)

Ask the Spirit to search your heart and reveal any areas of unconfessed sin. Acknowledge these to the Lord and thank Him for His forgiveness.

Renewal

O Lord my God, may I fear You, walk in all Your ways, love You, and serve You with all my heart and with all my soul. (Deuteronomy 10:12)

Christ Jesus, I have not been made perfect, but I press on to lay hold of that for which You laid hold of me. I do not consider myself yet to have attained it, but one thing I do: forgetting what is behind and stretching forward to what is ahead, I press on toward the goal to win the prize of the upward call of God in You. (Philippians 3:12–14)

Pause to add your own prayers for personal renewal.

Petition

My body is a temple of Your Holy Spirit, who is in me and whom I have received from You, Lord God. I am not my own, for I was bought at a price; therefore may I glorify You in my body. (1 Corinthians 6:19–20)

Pause here to petition God for growth in your desire to know and please Jesus Christ. Pray for a greater love and commitment to Him, for the grace to practice His presence and for the grace to glorify Him in your life. Offer prayers regarding your activities for this day and any special concerns you may have.

Intercession

We must take heed to ourselves and to all the flock of which Your Holy Spirit has made us overseers to shepherd Your church, which You, Jesus, purchased with Your own blood. (Acts 20:28)

Take a few moments to intercede on behalf of your local church, other churches, evangelism and discipleship ministries, educational ministries and any other special concerns you may have.

Affirmation

Your love, O Christ, compels me, because I am convinced that You are the One who died for all, and therefore all died. And You died for all, that those who live should no longer live for themselves but for the One who died for them and was raised again. (2 Corinthians 5:14–15)

You redeemed us from the curse of the law by becoming a curse for us, for it is written: "Cursed is everyone who hangs on a tree." (Galatians 3:13)

Pause to reflect on these Biblical affirmations.

Thanksgiving

In Your unfailing love You have led the people You have redeemed.
In Your strength You have guided them to Your holy dwelling.
You have brought them in and planted them on the mountain of Your inheritance—
The place, O Lord, You made for Your dwelling;
The sanctuary, O Lord, Your hands have established. (Exodus 15:13, 17)

You are the Lord our God, who brought Your people out of Egypt so that they would no longer be slaves; You broke the bars of their yoke and enabled them to walk with heads held high. (Leviticus 26:13)

Pause to offer your own expressions of thanksgiving.

Closing Prayer

Whom have I in heaven but You?
And there is nothing on earth I desire besides You.
My flesh and my heart may fail,

But You are the strength of my heart and my portion
  forever.
Those who are far from You will perish;
You have cut off all who are unfaithful to You.
But as for me, it is good to be near You.
I have made You, Lord God, my refuge,
That I may tell of all Your works. (Psalm 73:25–28)

DAY 2

Adoration

> How great are Your works, O Lord!
> Your thoughts are very deep.
> Senseless people do not know;
> Fools do not understand
> That though the wicked spring up like grass
> And all the evildoers flourish,
> They will be destroyed forever.
> But You, O Lord, are exalted forever. (Psalm 92:5–8)

> You are the Lord, that is Your name.
> You will not give Your glory to another
> Or Your praise to idols. (Isaiah 42:8)

Pause to express your thoughts of praise and worship.

Confession

I will endure discipline, for You are treating me as Your child. For what child is not disciplined by its father? If I am without discipline, of which all have become partakers, then I am an illegitimate child and not a true child. Moreover, we have all had human fathers who disciplined us, and we respected them; how much more should I be disciplined by You, the Father of my spirit, and live? (Hebrews 12:7–9)

Ask the Spirit to search your heart and reveal any areas of unconfessed sin. Acknowledge these to the Lord and thank Him for His forgiveness.

Renewal

O Christ, You must increase; I must decrease. (John 3:30)

Jesus, You are the true vine, and Your Father is the gardener. He cuts off every branch in You that bears no fruit, while every branch that does bear fruit He prunes, that it may bear more fruit. May I abide in You, and You in me. As the branch cannot bear fruit of itself, unless it abides in the vine, neither can I bear fruit unless I abide in You. (John 15:1–2, 4)

Pause to add your own prayers for personal renewal.

Petition

May I follow Abraham's example of willingness to offer all that I have to You, holding nothing back and trusting in Your character and in Your promises. (Genesis 22:2–12, 16)

Pause here to petition God for wisdom. Ask Him to develop your eternal perspective, to renew your mind with truth and to help you develop greater skill in each area of your life. Offer prayers regarding your activities for this day and any special concerns you may have.

Intercession

May we rejoice, become complete, be of good comfort, be of one mind, and live in peace; and You, the God of love and peace, will be with us. (2 Corinthians 13:11)

Take a few moments to intercede on behalf of your immediate family and other relatives. Offer prayers for their spiritual, emotional and physical concerns.

Affirmation

As I give, it will be given to me; a good measure, pressed down, shaken together and running over will be poured into my lap. For with the measure I use, it will be measured back to me. (Luke 6:38)

Those who sow sparingly will also reap sparingly, and those who sow bountifully will also reap bountifully. Each one should give as he has decided in his heart, not reluctantly or under compulsion; for You love a cheerful giver. And You are able to make all grace abound to us, so that always having all sufficiency in everything, we may abound in every good work. As it is written: "He has scattered abroad His gifts to the poor; His righteousness endures forever." Now You, the One who supplies seed to the sower and bread for food, will also supply and increase our seed and will increase the fruits of our righteousness. (2 Corinthians 9:6–10)

Pause to reflect on these Biblical affirmations.

Thanksgiving

We give thanks to You, Lord God Almighty, the One who is and who was, because You have taken Your great power and have begun to reign. (Revelation 11:17)

There will no longer be any curse. Your throne and the throne of the Lamb will be in the new Jerusalem, and Your servants will serve You. They will see Your face, and Your name will be on their foreheads. And there will be no night there; they will not need the light of a lamp or the light of the sun, for You, Lord God, will give them light. And they shall reign for ever and ever. (Revelation 22:3–5)

Pause to offer your own expressions of thanksgiving.

Closing Prayer

Blessed be Your name, Lord God, for ever and ever,
For wisdom and power belong to You.
You change the times and the seasons;
You raise up kings and depose them.
You give wisdom to the wise

And knowledge to those who have understanding.
You reveal deep and hidden things;
You know what is in the darkness,
And light dwells with You. (Daniel 2:20–22)

DAY 3

Adoration

> You, O Lord Most High, are awesome,
> The great King over all the earth!
> You are the King of all the earth,
> And I will sing Your praise.
> You reign over the nations;
> You are seated on Your holy throne. (Psalm 47:2, 7–8)

You must be treated as holy by those who come near You, and before all people You will be honored. (Leviticus 10:3)

Pause to express your thoughts of praise and worship.

Confession

> Lord, I have heard of Your fame, and I stand in awe of
>   Your deeds.
> O Lord, revive Your works in our day;
> In our time make them known;
> In wrath remember mercy. (Habakkuk 3:2)

Ask the Spirit to search your heart and reveal any areas of unconfessed sin. Acknowledge these to the Lord and thank Him for His forgiveness.

Renewal

Lord, may I not turn aside from following You, but serve You with all my heart. May I not turn aside to go after worthless things which do not profit or deliver me, because they are useless. (1 Samuel 12:20–21)

The works of the flesh are evident; they are immorality, impurity, sensuality, idolatry, sorcery, hatred, discord, jealousy, fits of rage, selfish ambition, dissensions, factions, envyings, drunkenness, revelries and the like. Those who practice such things will not inherit Your kingdom. But the fruit of the Spirit is love, joy, peace, patience, kindness, goodness, faithfulness, gentleness and self-control; against such things there is no law. (Galatians 5:19–23)

Pause to add your own prayers for personal renewal.

Petition

When I ask, it will be given to me; when I seek, I will find; when I knock, the door will be opened to me. For everyone who asks receives; everyone who seeks finds; and to everyone who knocks, the door will be opened. (Matthew 7:7–8; Luke 11:9–10)

Pause here to petition God for spiritual insight so that you might have understanding of His Word. Ask for insight into your identity in Jesus Christ: that you might know who you are, what direction your life should take and what His purpose for your life is. Offer prayers regarding your activities for this day and any special concerns you may have.

Intercession

You, Father, are my witness, whom I serve in my spirit in the gospel of Your Son, of how unceasingly I make mention of Your people in my prayers. (Romans 1:9)

Take a few moments to intercede on behalf of other believers, such as your personal friends, those in ministry and those who are oppressed and in need.

Affirmation

You, Lord, are a jealous God, punishing the children for the sin of the fathers to the third and fourth generation of those who hate You, but showing lovingkindness to a thousand generations of those who love You and keep Your commandments. (Exodus 20:5–6; Deuteronomy 5:9–10)

You are not a man, that You should lie, nor a son of man, that You should change Your mind. Have You spoken and not done it? Have You promised and not fulfilled it? (Numbers 23:19)

Pause to reflect on these Biblical affirmations.

Thanksgiving

I will remember Your works, O Lord;
Surely, I will remember Your wonders of long ago.
I will meditate on all Your works
And consider all Your mighty deeds.
Your way, O God, is holy.
What god is so great as You?
You are the God who works wonders;
You have revealed Your strength among the peoples.
You redeemed Your people with Your power,
The descendants of Jacob and Joseph. (Psalm 77:11–15)

Pause to offer your own expressions of thanksgiving.

Closing Prayer

O come, let us sing to You, Lord;
Let us shout joyfully to You, the Rock of our salvation.
Let us come before Your presence with thanksgiving;
Let us shout for joy to You with psalms. (Psalm 95:1–2)

We sing to You a new song;
Let all the earth sing to You.
We sing to You, Lord, and bless Your name;
We proclaim the good news of Your salvation day after
    day.
We declare Your glory among the nations,
Your marvelous works among all people. (Psalm 96:1–3)

Adoration

> You, O Lord, are great and greatly to be praised;
> You are to be feared above all gods.
> For all the gods of the nations are idols,
> But You made the heavens.
> Splendor and majesty are before You;
> Strength and joy are in Your place.
> I will ascribe to You glory and strength.
> I will ascribe to You the glory due Your name
> And worship You in the beauty of holiness.
> All the earth trembles before You.
> The world is firmly established, it will not be moved.
>   (1 Chronicles 16:25–30)

You are the God of Abraham and the Fear of Isaac. (Genesis 31:42)

Pause to express your thoughts of praise and worship.

Confession

> Save me from bloodguilt, O God,
> The God of my salvation,
> And my tongue will sing aloud of Your righteousness.
> O Lord, open my lips,
> And my mouth will declare Your praise.
> For You do not desire sacrifice, or I would bring it;
> You do not delight in burnt offerings.
> The sacrifices You desire are a broken spirit;
> A broken and contrite heart,
> O God, You will not despise. (Psalm 51:14–17)

Ask the Spirit to search your heart and reveal any areas of unconfessed sin. Acknowledge these to the Lord and thank Him for His forgiveness.

Renewal

May I remove the places of idolatry from my life, and like Asa, let my heart be fully committed to You all my days. (2 Chronicles 15:17)

> May I trust in You, Lord, and do good;
> May I dwell in the land and feed on Your faithfulness.
> When I delight myself in You,
> You will give me the desires of my heart.
> I will commit my way to You and trust in You,
> And You will bring it to pass.
> You will bring forth my righteousness like the light,
> And my justice like the noonday.
> May I rest in You and wait patiently for You;
> I will not fret because of those who prosper in their way,
> Because of those who practice evil schemes.
>   (Psalm 37:3–7)

Pause to add your own prayers for personal renewal.

Petition

May I not pervert justice, show partiality, or accept a bribe, for a bribe blinds the eyes of the wise and perverts the words of the righteous. (Deuteronomy 16:19)

Pause here to petition God for growth in love and compassion toward others. Offer prayers for your loved ones, for those who do not know Jesus and for those in need. Offer prayers regarding your activities for this day and any special concerns you may have.

Intercession

We are the fragrance of Christ to You, O God, among those
who are being saved and among those who are perishing; to
the one, we are an aroma from death to death; to the other,
an aroma from life to life. And who is sufficient for these
things? (2 Corinthians 2:15–16)

*Take a few moments to intercede on behalf of friends, relatives,
neighbors and coworkers who do not yet know salvation in Jesus
Christ.*

Affirmation

There is no one who has left house or brothers or sisters or
mother or father or children or fields for Your sake and the
gospel's, who will not receive a hundred times as much in
this present age—houses, brothers, sisters, mothers, children
and fields, along with persecutions—and in the age to come,
eternal life. (Matthew 19:29; Mark 10:29–30)

If anyone comes to You and does not hate his father and
mother, his wife and children, his brothers and sisters—yes,
even his own life—he cannot be Your disciple. And whoever does not carry his cross and follow You cannot be Your
disciple. (Luke 14:26–27)

Pause to reflect on these Biblical affirmations.

Thanksgiving

You have loved me with an everlasting love;
You have drawn me with lovingkindness. (Jeremiah 31:3)

You led Your people with cords of human kindness,
With bands of love;
You lifted the yoke from their neck
And bent down to feed them. (Hosea 11:4)

Pause to offer your own expressions of thanksgiving.

Closing Prayer

You are the Lord, the God of our fathers—the God of Abraham, the God of Isaac and the God of Jacob. This is Your name forever, the name by which You are to be remembered from generation to generation. (Exodus 3:15)

> I will sing to You, Lord, for You are highly exalted.
> You are my strength and my song;
> You have become my salvation.
> You are my God, and I will praise You,
> My father's God, and I will exalt You. (Exodus 15:1–2)

DAY 5

Adoration

Lord my God, You are God of gods and Lord of lords, the great God, mighty and awesome, who shows no partiality and accepts no bribes. You execute justice for the fatherless and the widow, and You love the alien, giving him food and clothing. (Deuteronomy 10:17–18)

> My soul magnifies You, Lord,
> And my spirit rejoices in You, my Savior,
> For You, O Mighty One, have done great things for me,
> And holy is Your name.
> Your mercy is on those who fear You,
> From generation to generation. (Luke 1:46–47, 49–50)

Pause to express your thoughts of praise and worship.

Confession

> Your eyes see the way people live,
> And You see all their steps.
> There is no darkness or deep shadow
> Where people who do evil can hide.
> You do not need to examine them further,
> That they should come before You in judgment.
>   (Job 34:21–23)

Ask the Spirit to search your heart and reveal any areas of unconfessed sin. Acknowledge these to the Lord and thank Him for His forgiveness.

Renewal

May I flee from sexual immorality. All other sins people

commit are outside their bodies, but sexually immoral people sin against their own bodies. (1 Corinthians 6:18)

May I not set my heart on evil things, or be an idolater or commit sexual immorality. (1 Corinthians 10:6–8)

Pause to add your own prayers for personal renewal.

Petition

> Let me hear Your unfailing love in the morning,
> For I have put my trust in You.
> Show me the way I should walk,
> For to You I lift up my soul. (Psalm 143:8)

Pause here to petition God to help you be a faithful steward of your time, talents, possessions and relationships. Offer prayers of petition regarding your activities for this day and any special concerns you may have.

Intercession

Lord, may I honor all people, love the community of believers, fear You, and honor the king. (1 Peter 2:17)

Take a few moments to intercede on behalf of your local, state or provincial, and national governments. Pray for spiritual revival in the nation and offer prayers regarding current events and concerns.

Affirmation

Your Scripture is God-breathed and is useful for teaching, for reproof, for correction and for training in righteousness, that we, Your people, may be thoroughly equipped for every good work. (2 Timothy 3:16–17)

We have the prophetic word made more certain, to which I will do well to pay attention, as to a light shining in a dark place, until the day dawns and the morning star rises in my heart. (2 Peter 1:19)

Pause to reflect on these Biblical affirmations.

Thanksgiving

You, Lord my God, /are the faithful God, who keeps Your covenant and Your lovingkindness to a thousand generations of those who love You and keep Your commands. (Deuteronomy 7:9)

> I will tell of Your lovingkindnesses, Lord,
> And praise Your deeds,
> According to all You have done for us,
> And Your great goodness toward the house of Israel,
> Which You have bestowed on them according to Your
>   mercies,
> And according to the multitude of Your
>   lovingkindnesses. (Isaiah 63:7)

Pause to offer your own expressions of thanksgiving.

Closing Prayer

> I know that You, my Redeemer, live
> And that in the end You will stand upon the earth.
> And after my skin has been destroyed,
> Yet in my flesh I will see You;
> I myself will see You
> And behold You with my own eyes and not another.
> How my heart yearns within me! (Job 19:25–27)

> You are exalted beyond our understanding, O God;
> The number of Your years is unsearchable. (Job 36:26)

Adoration

> Oh, the depth of the riches of Your wisdom and
>   knowledge!
> How unsearchable are Your judgments,
> And Your ways past finding out!
> For who has known Your mind, O Lord?
> Or who has been Your counselor?
> Or who has first given to You,
> That You should repay him?
> For from You and through You and to You are all things.
> To You be the glory forever! Amen. (Romans 11:33–36)

Hallelujah! Salvation and glory and power belong to You, our God, because Your judgments are true and righteous. (Revelation 19:1–2)

Pause to express your thoughts of praise and worship.

Confession

You, Lord my God, are gracious and compassionate, and You will not turn Your face from me if I return to You. (2 Chronicles 30:9)

Ask the Spirit to search your heart and reveal any areas of unconfessed sin. Acknowledge these to the Lord and thank Him for His forgiveness.

Renewal

Like Josiah, may I do what is right in Your sight, Lord. May I walk in the ways of David and not turn aside to the right or to the left. Give me a tender and responsive heart, so that

I will humble myself before You when I hear Your word. (2 Chronicles 34:1–2, 27)

Jesus, may I walk in Your steps, withdrawing to lonely places and praying to the Father. (Mark 1:35; Luke 5:16)

Pause to add your own prayers for personal renewal.

Petition

May my conscience testify that I have conducted myself in the world in the holiness and sincerity that are from You, not in fleshly wisdom but in Your grace, especially in my relationships with others. (2 Corinthians 1:12)

Pause here to offer prayers of petition regarding your family and your ministry. Ask for help and guidance in sharing Jesus with others and helping others grow in Him. Ask for guidance in your vocation and your avocations. Offer prayers of petition regarding your activities for this day and any special concerns you may have.

Intercession

Remember us, O my God, and do not blot out what we have done in Your name. Remember us, O my God, for good. (Nehemiah 13:14, 31)

Take a few moments to intercede on behalf of local, national and world missions. Pray that the Great Commission would be fulfilled and for any special concerns you may have for missions.

Affirmation

The hour is coming and now is, when true worshipers will worship You, Father, in spirit and truth, for You are seeking such to worship You. You are spirit, and those who worship You must worship in spirit and truth. (John 4:23–24)

Jesus, those who obey Your commandments abide in You, and You in them. And this is how I know that You abide in me: by the Spirit whom You have given me. (1 John 3:24)

Pause to reflect on these Biblical affirmations.

Thanksgiving

We know Your grace, Lord Jesus Christ, that though You were rich, yet for our sakes You became poor, that through Your poverty we might become rich. (2 Corinthians 8:9)

O God, we thank You for Your indescribable gift! (2 Corinthians 9:15)

Pause to offer your own expressions of thanksgiving.

Closing Prayer

I will not fear, for You are with me;
I will not be dismayed, for You are my God.
You will strengthen me and help me;
You will uphold me with Your righteous right hand.
For You are the Lord my God, who takes hold of my
   right hand
And says to me, "Do not fear; I will help you."
   (Isaiah 41:10, 13)

I call this to mind,
And therefore I have hope:
Your mercies never cease,
For Your compassions never fail.
They are new every morning;
Great is Your faithfulness. (Lamentations 3:21–23)

DAY 7

Adoration

Lord my God, You are God in the heavens above and in the earth below. (Joshua 2:11)

> You stretch out the north over empty space;
> You suspend the earth on nothing. (Job 26:7)

> You made the Pleiades and Orion
> And turn deep darkness into morning
> And darken day into night.
> You call for the waters of the sea
> And pour them out over the face of the earth—
> The Lord is Your name. (Amos 5:8)

Pause to express your thoughts of praise and worship.

Confession

My Lord, let Your power be great, just as You have spoken, saying, "The Lord is slow to anger and abounding in mercy, forgiving iniquity and transgression." (Numbers 14:17–18)

Ask the Spirit to search your heart and reveal any areas of unconfessed sin. Acknowledge these to the Lord and thank Him for His forgiveness.

Renewal

May Your name, Lord Jesus, be magnified in my life. (Acts 19:17)

In view of Your mercy, O God, may I present my body as a living sacrifice, holy and pleasing to You, which is my reasonable service. (Romans 12:1)

Pause to add your own prayers for personal renewal.

Petition

May I do no injustice in judgment, nor show partiality to the poor or favoritism to the great, but judge my neighbor fairly. (Leviticus 19:15)

Pause here to petition God for growth in your character and personal discipline, and for physical health and strength. Ask that He empower you for spiritual warfare against the temptations of the world, the flesh and the devil. Offer prayers regarding your activities for this day and any special concerns you may have.

Intercession

> O Lord, be gracious to us; we have hoped in You.
> Be our strength every morning,
> Our salvation in time of distress. (Isaiah 33:2)

Take a few moments to intercede on behalf of the poor and hungry, the oppressed and persecuted, and those in control of world and national resources. Offer prayers for peace among nations and regarding current events and concerns.

Affirmation

> Blessed is the one who finds wisdom
> And the one who gains understanding,
> For wisdom's profit is greater than that of silver,
> And her gain is more than fine gold.
> She is more precious than jewels,
> And nothing I desire can compare with her.
> Long life is in her right hand;
> In her left hand are riches and honor.
> Her ways are pleasant ways,
> And all her paths are peace.
> She is a tree of life to those who embrace her,
> And happy are those who hold her fast.
>   (Proverbs 3:13–18)

Wisdom is foremost; therefore I will get wisdom,
And though it costs all I have, I will get understanding.
I will esteem her, and she will exalt me;
I will embrace her, and she will honor me.
  (Proverbs 4:7–8)

Pause to reflect on these Biblical affirmations.

Thanksgiving

Has any other people heard Your voice speaking out of the midst of the fire, as the children of Israel have, and lived? Has any god ever tried to take for himself one nation from the midst of another nation by trials, by miraculous signs and wonders, by war, by a mighty hand and an outstretched arm, and by great and awesome deeds, like all the things You, Lord God, did for Israel in Egypt before their very eyes? The Israelites were shown these things so that they might know that You are the Lord God; there is no other besides You. Out of heaven You made the children of Israel hear Your voice to discipline them. On earth You showed them Your great fire, and they heard Your words out of the midst of the fire. Because You loved their fathers, You chose their descendants after them, and You brought them out of Egypt by Your presence and Your great power; You drove out from before the Israelites nations greater and mightier than they, to bring them in and to give them their land as an inheritance. (Deuteronomy 4:33–38)

Pause to offer your own expressions of thanksgiving.

Closing Prayer

Lord Jesus, I have nowhere else to go; You have the words of eternal life. I believe and know that You are the Holy One of God. (John 6:68–69)

You are the resurrection and the life. Those who believe in You will live, even though they die, and those who live and believe in You will never die. (John 11:25–26)

DAY 8

Adoration

> You, the Lord, alone have declared
> What is to come from the distant past.
> There is no God apart from You,
> A righteous God and a Savior;
> There is none besides You.
> You are God, and there is no other. (Isaiah 45:21–22)

> You are my hope, O Lord God;
> You are my trust from my youth.
> As for me, I will always have hope;
> I will praise You more and more. (Psalm 71:5, 14)

Pause to express your thoughts of praise and worship.

Confession

> You are not a God who takes pleasure in wickedness;
> Evil cannot dwell with You. (Psalm 5:4)

Ask the Spirit to search your heart and reveal any areas of unconfessed sin. Acknowledge these to the Lord and thank Him for His forgiveness.

Renewal

Like Enoch, may I walk with You. (Genesis 5:24)

Like Noah, may I find favor in Your eyes, O Lord. (Genesis 6:8)

Pause to add your own prayers for personal renewal.

Petition

May I consider the members of my earthly body as dead to
immorality, impurity, passion, evil desires and greed, which
is idolatry. Because of these, O God, Your wrath is coming.
I used to walk in these ways, in the life I once lived. (Colossians 3:5–7)

*Pause here to petition God for growth in your desire to know
and please Jesus Christ. Pray for a greater love and commitment
to Him, for the grace to practice His presence and for the grace
to glorify Him in your life. Offer prayers regarding your activities
for this day and any special concerns you may have.*

Intercession

We have many parts in one body, but all the parts do not
have the same function; in the same way, we who are many
are one body in You, Christ Jesus, and individually members
of one another. And we have different gifts, according
to the grace You have given to us. (Romans 12:4–6)

*Take a few moments to intercede on behalf of your local church,
other churches, evangelism and discipleship ministries, educational
ministries and any other special concerns you may have.*

Affirmation

I believe that it is through Your grace, Lord Jesus, that I am
saved. (Acts 15:11)

Jesus, I trusted in You when I heard the word of truth, the
gospel of my salvation. Having believed, I was sealed in You
with the Holy Spirit of promise, who is a deposit guaranteeing my inheritance until the redemption of those who are
the Father's possession, to the praise of His glory. (Ephesians
1:13–14)

Pause to reflect on these Biblical affirmations.

Thanksgiving

I will sing of Your mercies, Lord, forever;
With my mouth I will make Your faithfulness known
    through all generations.
I will declare that Your lovingkindness will be built up
    forever,
That You will establish Your faithfulness in the heavens.
And the heavens will praise Your wonders, O Lord,
Your faithfulness also in the assembly of the holy ones.
For who in the heavens can be compared with You?
Who is like You among the children of the mighty?
You are greatly feared in the council of the holy ones
And more awesome than all who surround You.
O Lord God of hosts, who is like You, O mighty Lord?
Your faithfulness also surrounds You.
    (Psalm 89:1–2, 5–8)

Pause to offer your own expressions of thanksgiving.

Closing Prayer

Jesus, You are the living bread that came down from heaven.
Those who eat of this bread will live forever. This bread is
Your flesh, which You have given for the life of the world.
(John 6:51)

You are the light of the world. Those who follow You will
not walk in the darkness but will have the light of life. (John
8:12)

DAY 9

Adoration

> Lord, You have been our dwelling place throughout all
>   generations.
> Before the mountains were born
> Or You brought forth the earth and the world;
> From everlasting to everlasting You are God.
> You turn people back into dust
> And say, "Return to dust."
> For a thousand years in Your sight
> Are like yesterday when it passes by
> Or like a watch in the night. (Psalm 90:1–4)

Lord Jesus Christ, You are the same yesterday, today, and forever. (Hebrews 13:8)

Pause to express your thoughts of praise and worship.

Confession

> You, O God, fashion the hearts of all
> And understand all their works. (Psalm 33:15)

Ask the Spirit to search your heart and reveal any areas of unconfessed sin. Acknowledge these to the Lord and thank Him for His forgiveness.

Renewal

> Has a nation changed its gods
> That were not gods?
> But Your people have exchanged their Glory
> For that which is worthless.
> By Your grace may I not forsake You,

The fountain of living waters,
To dig my own cisterns,
Broken cisterns that can hold no water. (Jeremiah 2:11, 13)

As one who shares in the heavenly calling, may I fix my thoughts on You, Jesus, the Apostle and High Priest of my confession. (Hebrews 3:1)

Pause to add your own prayers for personal renewal.

Petition

May I be strong and courageous and careful to obey Your word; may I not turn from it to the right or to the left, that I may act wisely wherever I go. (Joshua 1:7)

Pause here to petition God for wisdom. Ask Him to develop your eternal perspective, to renew your mind with truth and to help you develop greater skill in each area of your life. Offer prayers regarding your activities for this day and any special concerns you may have.

Intercession

We should bear with one another in love, and make every effort to keep the unity of the Spirit in the bond of peace. (Ephesians 4:2–3)

Take a few moments to intercede on behalf of your immediate family and other relatives. Offer prayers for their spiritual, emotional and physical concerns.

Affirmation

Naked I came from my mother's womb,
And naked I will depart.
Lord, You give and You take away;
Blessed be Your name, O Lord. (Job 1:21)

Godliness with contentment is great gain. For I brought nothing into the world, and I can take nothing out of it. But if I have food and clothing, with these I will be content. (1 Timothy 6:6–8)

Pause to reflect on these Biblical affirmations.

Thanksgiving

> I called to You in my distress, O Lord,
> And You answered me.
> From the depths of the grave I called for help,
> And You heard my voice. (Jonah 2:2)

> I will exult in You, O Lord;
> I will rejoice in You, the God of my salvation.
> You are my strength;
> You make my feet like the feet of a deer
> And enable me to go on the heights.
>   (Habakkuk 3:18–19)

Pause to offer your own expressions of thanksgiving.

Closing Prayer

Lord Jesus, You are the door; whoever enters through You will be saved and will come in and go out and find pasture. The thief comes only to steal and kill and destroy; You have come that we may have life and have it abundantly. (John 10:9–10)

Jesus, Your sheep hear Your voice, and You know them, and they follow You. You give them eternal life, and they shall never perish; no one can snatch them out of Your hand. The Father, who has given them to You, is greater than all; no one can snatch them out of the Father's hand. You and the Father are one. (John 10:27–30)

DAY 10

Adoration

I will exalt You, my God and King;
I will bless Your name for ever and ever.
Every day I will bless You,
And I will praise Your name for ever and ever.
Great are You, Lord, and most worthy of praise;
Your greatness is unsearchable. (Psalm 145:1–3)

Out of the north You come in golden splendor;
With You is awesome majesty.
You, the Almighty, are beyond our reach;
You are exalted in power,
And in Your justice and great righteousness,
You do not oppress. (Job 37:22–23)

Pause to express your thoughts of praise and worship.

Confession

You, O God, will not always strive with us,
Nor will You harbor Your anger forever;
You do not treat us as our sins deserve
Or repay us according to our iniquities.
For as high as the heavens are above the earth,
So great is Your love for those who fear You;
As far as the east is from the west,
So far have You removed our transgressions from us.
As a father has compassion on his children,
So You have compassion on those who fear You.
    (Psalm 103:9–13)

*Ask the Spirit to search your heart and reveal any areas of
unconfessed sin. Acknowledge these to the Lord and thank Him
for His forgiveness.*

Renewal

May I have respect for You, Lord, and serve You faithfully.
May I do it with all my heart. (2 Chronicles 19:7)

> May I meditate on Your precepts
> And consider Your ways.
> May I delight in Your statutes,
> And not forget Your word.
> Deal bountifully with Your servant,
> That I may live and keep Your word.
> Open my eyes that I may see
> Wonderful things from Your law. (Psalm 119:15–18)

Pause to add your own prayers for personal renewal.

Petition

> May I not enter the path of the wicked
> Or walk in the way of evil men. (Proverbs 4:14)

*Pause here to petition God for spiritual insight so that you might
have understanding of His Word. Ask for insight into your identity in Jesus Christ: that you might know who you are, what
direction your life should take and what His purpose for your life
is. Offer prayers regarding your activities for this day and any
special concerns you may have.*

Intercession

Holy Spirit, help me in my weakness, for I do not know
what I ought to pray for, but You Yourself intercede for me
with groans that words cannot express. And He who searches
my heart knows Your mind, because You intercede for the
saints according to the Father's will. (Romans 8:26–27)

*Take a few moments to intercede on behalf of other believers,
such as your personal friends, those in ministry and those who
are oppressed and in need.*

Affirmation

Jesus, You rejoiced in the Holy Spirit and said, "I praise You, Father, Lord of heaven and earth, because You have hidden these things from the wise and learned, and revealed them to little children. Yes, Father, for this was well-pleasing in Your sight. All things have been delivered to Me by You, Father. No one knows the Son except You, and no one knows You except the Son and those to whom the Son chooses to reveal You." (Matthew 11:25–27; Luke 10:21–22)

Your foolishness, O God, is wiser than human wisdom, and Your weakness is stronger than human strength. But You chose the foolish things of the world to shame the wise, and You chose the weak things of the world to shame the strong; and the lowly things of this world and the despised things You have chosen, and the things that are not, to nullify the things that are, so that no one may boast before You. (1 Corinthians 1:25, 27–29)

Pause to reflect on these Biblical affirmations.

Thanksgiving

As the Israelites rejoiced, may I also rejoice in You, O God:

> Rejoice greatly, O daughter of Zion!
> Shout, O daughter of Jerusalem!
> Behold, Your King is coming to you;
> He is just and having salvation,
> Humble and riding on a donkey,
> On a colt, the foal of a donkey.
> He will proclaim peace to the nations;
> His dominion will extend from sea to sea
> And from the River to the ends of the earth.
> (Zechariah 9:9–10)

Pause to offer your own expressions of thanksgiving.

Closing Prayer

O Lord, bless us and keep us;
O Lord, make Your face shine upon us
And be gracious to us;
O Lord, turn Your face toward us
And give us peace. (Numbers 6:24–26)

DAY 11

Adoration

O Lord, God of Israel, there is no God like You in heaven above or on earth below; You keep Your covenant and mercy with Your servants who walk before You with all their heart.ʳ (1 Kings 8:23; 2 Chronicles 6:14)

> I know that You alone, whose name is the Lord,
> Are the Most High over all the earth. (Psalm 83:18)

Pause to express your thoughts of praise and worship.

Confession

> A person's wickedness will punish him;
> His backsliding will reprove him.
> I know, therefore, and see that it is evil and bitter
> To forsake You, the Lord my God,
> And have no fear of You. (Jeremiah 2:19)

Ask the Spirit to search your heart and reveal any areas of unconfessed sin. Acknowledge these to the Lord and thank Him for His forgiveness.

Renewal

May I be anxious for nothing, but in everything, by prayer and petition with thanksgiving, let my requests be known to You, O God. And may Your peace, which transcends all understanding, guard my heart and my mind in Christ Jesus. (Philippians 4:6–7)

May I prepare my mind for action and be self-controlled, setting my hope fully on the grace to be given to me at Your revelation, Christ Jesus. (1 Peter 1:13)

Pause to add your own prayers for personal renewal.

Petition

Lord, may I not be ashamed to testify about You, but join with others in suffering for the gospel according to Your power. (2 Timothy 1:8)

Pause here to petition God for growth in love and compassion toward others. Offer prayers for your loved ones, for those who do not know Jesus and for those in need. Offer prayers regarding your activities for this day and any special concerns you may have.

Intercession

The god of this age has blinded the minds of unbelievers, so that they cannot see the light of the gospel of Your glory, O Christ, You who are the image of God. (2 Corinthians 4:4)

Take a few moments to intercede on behalf of friends, relatives, neighbors and coworkers who do not yet know salvation in Jesus Christ.

Affirmation

Lord Jesus Christ, You have been raised from the dead, the firstfruits of those who have fallen asleep. For since death came through a man, the resurrection of the dead comes also through a Man. For as in Adam all die, so in You all will be made alive. But each in his own order: You, the firstfruits; afterward, those who are Yours at Your coming. Then the end will come, when You deliver the kingdom to God the Father, after You have abolished all rule and all authority and power. For You must reign until You have put all Your enemies under Your feet. The last enemy that will be destroyed is death. (1 Corinthians 15:20–26)

The first man was of the dust of the earth; You, O Jesus, the second Man, are from heaven. As was the earthly man, so are those who are of the earth; and as You, the Man from heaven, are, so also are those who are of heaven. And just as we have borne the image of the earthly man, so shall we bear Your likeness, You who are the heavenly Man. (1 Corinthians 15:47–49)

Pause to reflect on these Biblical affirmations.

Thanksgiving

Jesus, You who are the Son of Man did not come to be served, but to serve, and to give Your life as a ransom for many. (Matthew 20:28)

Jesus, we remember that You took bread, gave thanks, and broke it, and gave it to Your disciples, saying, "Take and eat; this is My body." Then You took the cup, gave thanks, and offered it to them, saying, "Drink from it, all of you. This is My blood of the new covenant, which is poured out for many for the forgiveness of sins." (Matthew 26:26–28)

Pause to offer your own expressions of thanksgiving.

Closing Prayer

I will arise and bless You, Lord my God;
You are from everlasting to everlasting.
Blessed be Your glorious name,
Which is exalted above all blessing and praise!
   (Nehemiah 9:5)

As for me, I will see Your face in righteousness;
When I awake, I will be satisfied with Your likeness.
   (Psalm 17:15)

Adoration

> You are a jealous and avenging God;
> You take vengeance and are filled with wrath.
> You take vengeance on Your adversaries,
> And You reserve wrath against Your enemies.
> You are slow to anger and great in power
> And will not leave the guilty unpunished.
> Your way is in the whirlwind and the storm,
> And clouds are the dust of Your feet. (Nahum 1:2–3)

> Are You a God nearby,
> And not a God far away?
> Can anyone hide in secret places
> So that You cannot see him?
> Do You not fill heaven and earth? (Jeremiah 23:23–24)

Pause to express your thoughts of praise and worship.

Confession

> To fear You, Lord, is to hate evil;
> Wisdom hates pride and arrogance
> And the evil way and the perverse mouth.
>   (Proverbs 8:13)

Ask the Spirit to search your heart and reveal any areas of unconfessed sin. Acknowledge these to the Lord and thank Him for His forgiveness.

Renewal

May I not trust in myself or in my own righteousness nor view others with contempt. (Luke 18:9)

May I not be like those who do not make You their strength but trust in the abundance of their wealth and strengthen themselves in their evil desires. (Psalm 52:7)

Pause to add your own prayers for personal renewal.

Petition

> Turn to me and be gracious to me,
> For I am lonely and afflicted.
> The troubles of my heart have multiplied;
> Free me from my distresses.
> Look on my affliction and my pain
> And forgive all my sins. (Psalm 25:16–18)

Pause here to petition God to help you be a faithful steward of your time, talents, possessions and relationships. Offer prayers of petition regarding your activities for this day and any special concerns you may have.

Intercession

May I remind others to be subject to rulers and authorities, to be obedient, to be ready for every good work, to slander no one, to be peaceable and gentle, and to show true humility toward all people. (Titus 3:1–2)

Take a few moments to intercede on behalf of your local, state or provincial, and national governments. Pray for spiritual revival in the nation and offer prayers regarding current events and concerns.

Affirmation

I am always of good courage and know that as long as I am at home in the body, I am away from You, Lord. For I live by faith, not by sight. I am of good courage and would pre-

fer to be absent from the body and to be at home with You.
(2 Corinthians 5:6–8)

Now I am Your child, Father, and what I shall be has not yet
been revealed. I know that when Christ is revealed, I shall
be like Him, for I shall see Him as He is. And everyone who
has this hope in Him purifies himself, just as He is pure.
(1 John 3:2–3)

Pause to reflect on these Biblical affirmations.

Thanksgiving

Praise be to You, the God of Israel,
Because You have visited us and have redeemed Your
    people.
You have raised up a horn of salvation for us
In the house of Your servant David
(As You spoke by the mouth of Your holy prophets of
    long ago),
Salvation from our enemies
And from the hand of all who hate us—
To show mercy to our fathers
And to remember Your holy covenant,
The oath You swore to our father Abraham:
To rescue us from the hand of our enemies,
And to enable us to serve You without fear
In holiness and righteousness before You all our days.
    (Luke 1:68–75)

Pause to offer your own expressions of thanksgiving.

Closing Prayer

Your law, O Lord, is perfect, restoring the soul.
Your testimony is sure, making wise the simple.
Your precepts are right, rejoicing the heart.

Your commandments are pure, enlightening the eyes.
To fear You is pure, enduring forever.
Your judgments are true and altogether righteous.
They are more desirable than gold, than much pure gold;
They are sweeter than honey, than honey from the comb.
Moreover, by them is Your servant warned;
In keeping them there is great reward. (Psalm 19:7–11)

DAY 13

Adoration

> O Lord, You have searched me and You know me.
> You know when I sit down and when I rise up;
> You understand my thoughts from afar.
> You scrutinize my path and my lying down
> And are acquainted with all my ways.
> Before a word is on my tongue,
> O Lord, You know it completely.
> You have enclosed me behind and before,
> And laid Your hand upon me.
> Such knowledge is too wonderful for me;
> It is too lofty for me to attain. (Psalm 139:1–6)

Pause to express your thoughts of praise and worship.

Confession

> O Lord, be gracious to me;
> Heal my soul, for I have sinned against You.
>   (Psalm 41:4)

Ask the Spirit to search your heart and reveal any areas of unconfessed sin. Acknowledge these to the Lord and thank Him for His forgiveness.

Renewal

May I not worry about my life, what I will eat or what I will drink; or about my body, what I will wear. Life is more than food, and the body more than clothes. The birds of the air do not sow or reap or gather into barns, and yet You, my heavenly Father, feed them. Am I not much more valuable than they? Can I add a single hour to my life by worrying? And why do I worry about clothes? I will consider how the lilies of the field grow; they neither labor nor spin, yet not even Solomon in all his splendor was dressed like one of these. But if You so clothe the grass of the field, which is here today and tomorrow is thrown into the fire, will You not much more clothe me? So may I not worry, saying, "What shall I eat?" or "What shall I drink?" or "What shall I wear?" For the pagans run after all these things, and You, my heavenly Father, know that I need them. But may I seek first Your kingdom and Your righteousness, and all these things will be added to me. (Matthew 6:25–33; Luke 12:22–31)

May I be more concerned about the things of God than the things of men. (Mark 8:33)

Pause to add your own prayers for personal renewal.

Petition

May I follow Your commands and precepts and be careful to observe them, for this is my wisdom and understanding in the sight of others. (Deuteronomy 4:5–6)

Pause here to offer prayers of petition regarding your family and your ministry. Ask for help and guidance in sharing Jesus with others and helping others grow in Him. Ask for guidance in your vocation and your avocations. Offer prayers of petition regarding your activities for this day and any special concerns you may have.

Intercession

But let all who take refuge in You be glad;
Let them ever sing for joy
Because You defend them.
And let those who love Your name be joyful in You.
    (Psalm 5:11)

Take a few moments to intercede on behalf of local, national and world missions. Pray that the Great Commission would be fulfilled and for any special concerns you may have for missions.

Affirmation

> To fear You, Lord, that is wisdom,
> And to depart from evil is understanding. (Job 28:28)

> Who are those that fear You?
> You will instruct them in the way they should choose.
>   (Psalm 25:12)

> Blessed is everyone who fears You, Lord,
> And who walks in Your ways. (Psalm 128:1)

> You take pleasure in those who fear You, O Lord,
> Who put their hope in Your unfailing love.
>   (Psalm 147:11)

Pause to reflect on these Biblical affirmations.

Thanksgiving

I thank You, Lord Jesus, for Your promises: "I will see you again and your hearts will rejoice, and no one will take your joy from you. And in that day you will not ask Me any question. I tell you the truth, whatever you ask the Father in My name He will give you . . . ask, and you will receive, that your joy may be full." (John 16:22–24)

You, Father, love me because I have loved Jesus and have believed that He came forth from You. (John 16:27)

Pause to offer your own expressions of thanksgiving.

Closing Prayer

> You have shown me what is good;
> And what do You require of me

But to act justly and to love mercy
And to walk humbly with You, my God? (Micah 6:8)

We will all stand before Your judgment seat, O God. For it
is written:

"As I live, says the Lord, every knee will bow before Me,
And every tongue will confess to God."
So then, each of us will give an account to You.
    (Romans 14:10–12)

Adoration

> Where can I go from Your Spirit?
> Or where can I flee from Your presence?
> If I ascend to heaven, You are there;
> If I make my bed in Sheol, You are there.
> If I take the wings of the dawn,
> If I dwell in the depths of the sea,
> Even there Your hand will lead me;
> Your right hand will lay hold of me.
> If I say, "Surely the darkness will cover me,"
> Even the night will be light around me.
> The darkness is not dark to You,
> And the night shines as the day;
> Darkness and light are alike to You. (Psalm 139:7–12)

Pause to express your thoughts of praise and worship.

Confession

Those whom You love, You rebuke and discipline. Therefore may I be zealous and repent. (Revelation 3:19)

Ask the Spirit to search your heart and reveal any areas of unconfessed sin. Acknowledge these to the Lord and thank Him for His forgiveness.

Renewal

May I act in the fear of You, Lord, faithfully and with a loyal heart. (2 Chronicles 19:9)

> Teach me Your way, O Lord;
> I will walk in Your truth;
> Unite my heart to fear Your name. (Psalm 86:11)

Your foremost commandment is this: "Hear, O Israel; the Lord our God, the Lord is one; and you shall love the Lord your God with all your heart and with all your soul and with all your mind and with all your strength." The second is this: "You shall love your neighbor as yourself." There is no commandment greater than these. To love You with all my heart and with all my understanding and with all my strength, and to love my neighbor as myself are more important than all burnt offerings and sacrifices. (Mark 12:29–31, 33)

Pause to add your own prayers for personal renewal.

Petition

May I be strong and courageous, and act. May I not be afraid or discouraged, for You, Lord God, are with me. You will not fail me or forsake me. (1 Chronicles 28:20)

Pause here to petition God for growth in your character and personal discipline, and for physical health and strength. Ask that He empower you for spiritual warfare against the temptations of the world, the flesh and the devil. Offer prayers regarding your activities for this day and any special concerns you may have.

Intercession

O Lord, I know that You will maintain the cause of the afflicted
And justice for the poor. (Psalm 140:12)

Take a few moments to intercede on behalf of the poor and hungry, the oppressed and persecuted, and those in control of world and national resources. Offer prayers for peace among nations and regarding current events and concerns.

Affirmation

O God our Father, those You foreknew, You also predestined to be conformed to the likeness of Your Son, that He might be the firstborn among many brothers and sisters. And those You predestined, You also called; those You called, You also justified; those You justified, You also glorified. (Romans 8:29–30)

If I confess with my mouth the Lord Jesus and believe in my heart that You raised Him from the dead, I will be saved. For it is with my heart that I believe unto righteousness, and it is with my mouth that I confess unto salvation. As the Scripture says, "Whoever trusts in Him will not be put to shame." (Romans 10:9–11)

Pause to reflect on these Biblical affirmations.

Thanksgiving

At just the right time, when we were helpless, Christ died for the ungodly. For rarely will anyone die for a righteous man, though perhaps for a good man someone would even dare to die. But You demonstrate Your own love for us in that while we were still sinners, Christ died for us, O God. (Romans 5:6–8)

Since I have been justified by Christ's blood, much more shall I be saved from Your wrath through Him. For if, when I was Your enemy, I was reconciled to You through the death of Your Son, much more, having been reconciled, shall I be saved through His life. And not only this, but I also rejoice in You through my Lord Jesus Christ, through whom I have now received reconciliation. (Romans 5:9–11)

Pause to offer your own expressions of thanksgiving.

Closing Prayer

Lord Jesus, You are the Alpha and the Omega, the Beginning and the End. To anyone who is thirsty, You will give to drink without cost from the spring of the water of life. Those who overcome will inherit all this, and You will be their God and they will be Your children. (Revelation 21:6–7)

Lord Jesus, You are coming quickly. Your reward is with You, and You will give to everyone according to what he has done. You are the Alpha and the Omega, the First and the Last, the Beginning and the End. Yes, You are coming quickly. Amen. Come, Lord Jesus! (Revelation 22:12–13, 20)

Adoration

You formed my inward parts;
You wove me together in my mother's womb.
I thank You because I am fearfully and wonderfully
    made;
Your works are wonderful,
And my soul knows it full well.
My frame was not hidden from You
When I was made in secret
And skillfully wrought in the depths of the earth.
Your eyes saw my embryo,
And all the days ordained for me
Were written in Your book
Before one of them came to be. (Psalm 139:13–16)

Pause to express your thoughts of praise and worship.

Confession

I return to You, Lord my God,
For I have stumbled because of my iniquity.
I take words with me and return to You,
Saying, "Take away all iniquity and receive me
    graciously,
That I may offer the fruit of my lips." (Hosea 14:1–2)

*Ask the Spirit to search your heart and reveal any areas of
unconfessed sin. Acknowledge these to the Lord and thank Him
for His forgiveness.*

Renewal

God, I pray that You, according to the riches of Your glory,
would strengthen me with power through Your Spirit in

my inner being, so that Christ may dwell in my heart through faith. And may I, being rooted and grounded in love, be able to comprehend with all the saints what is the width and length and height and depth of the love of Christ, and to know this love that surpasses knowledge, that I may be filled to the measure of all Your fullness. (Ephesians 3:16–19)

May I be strong in the grace that is in You, Christ Jesus. (2 Timothy 2:1)

Pause to add your own prayers for personal renewal.

Petition

I was once darkness, but now I am light in You, Lord. May I walk as a child of light (for the fruit of the light consists in all goodness and righteousness and truth), learning what is pleasing to You. (Ephesians 5:8–10)

Pause here to petition God for growth in your desire to know and please Jesus Christ. Pray for a greater love and commitment to Him, for the grace to practice His presence and for the grace to glorify Him in your life. Offer prayers regarding your activities for this day and any special concerns you may have.

Intercession

How good and pleasant it is
When brothers and sisters live together in unity!
(Psalm 133:1)

Take a few moments to intercede on behalf of your local church, other churches, evangelism and discipleship ministries, educational ministries and any other special concerns you may have.

Affirmation

Father, those who are in Christ, Your Son, are new creations; the old things passed away; behold, they have become new. (2 Corinthians 5:17)

We are the true circumcision, we who worship by Your Spirit and glory in Christ Jesus and put no confidence in the flesh. (Philippians 3:3)

The mystery that has been kept hidden for ages and generations is now disclosed to the saints. O God, to them You have chosen to make known among the Gentiles the glorious riches of this mystery, which is Christ in us, the hope of glory. (Colossians 1:26–27)

Pause to reflect on these Biblical affirmations.

Thanksgiving

I am unworthy of all the lovingkindness and faithfulness You have shown Your servant. (Genesis 32:10)

You are the God who answered me in the day of my distress and have been with me wherever I have gone. (Genesis 35:3)

God Almighty, You are my shepherd, the Rock of Israel, who helps me and blesses me with blessings of the heavens above. (Genesis 49:24–25)

Pause to offer your own expressions of thanksgiving.

Closing Prayer

You are the great God,
The great King above all gods.
In Your hand are the depths of the earth,
And the summits of the mountains are Yours also.
The sea is Yours, for You made it,

And Your hands formed the dry land.
You are our God and we are the people of Your pasture
And the sheep under Your care. (Psalm 95:3–5, 7)

All the earth shouts joyfully to You, O Lord.
We worship You with gladness.
We come before You with joyful singing.
You, O Lord, are God.
It is You who made us, and not we ourselves;
We are Your people and the sheep of Your pasture.
   (Psalm 100:1–3)

DAY 16

Adoration

How precious are Your thoughts to me, O God!
How vast is the sum of them!
If I should count them, they would outnumber the
grains of sand.
When I awake, I am still with You. (Psalm 139:17–18)

To whom can I liken You or count You equal?
To whom can I compare You that You may be alike?
(Isaiah 46:5)

Pause to express your thoughts of praise and worship.

Confession

My trespasses are multiplied before You,
And my sins testify against me.
For my transgressions are with me,
And I know my iniquities:
Transgressing and lying against You, O Lord,
Turning my back on You,
Speaking oppression and revolt,
Uttering lies my heart has conceived. (Isaiah 59:12–13)

*Ask the Spirit to search your heart and reveal any areas of
unconfessed sin. Acknowledge these to the Lord and thank Him
for His forgiveness.*

Renewal

May I fear You, Lord, and serve You in truth with all my
heart, for I consider what great things You have done for me.
(1 Samuel 12:24)

May I not transgress Your commandments, Lord, for I cannot prosper in disobedience. May I not forsake You. (2 Chronicles 24:20)

Pause to add your own prayers for personal renewal.

Petition

May I be worthy of respect, not double-tongued, not addicted to wine, not fond of dishonest gain, but holding the mystery of the faith with a clear conscience. (1 Timothy 3:8–9)

Pause here to petition God for wisdom. Ask Him to develop your eternal perspective, to renew your mind with truth and to help you develop greater skill in each area of your life. Offer prayers regarding your activities for this day and any special concerns you may have.

Intercession

Father, I pray that Your beloved children may prosper in all things and be in good health, even as their souls prosper. (3 John 2)

Take a few moments to intercede on behalf of your immediate family and other relatives. Offer prayers for their spiritual, emotional and physical concerns.

Affirmation

You, O Christ, have appeared once for all at the end of the ages to do away with sin by sacrificing Yourself. And as it is appointed for people to die once and after that to face judgment, so You were offered once to bear the sins of many; and You will appear a second time, not to bear sin but to bring salvation to those who eagerly wait for You. (Hebrews 9:26–28)

O Jesus, You were chosen before the creation of the world
but were revealed in these last times for my sake. Through
You I believe in God the Father, who raised You from the
dead and glorified You, so that my faith and hope are in
Almighty God. (1 Peter 1:20–21)

Pause to reflect on these Biblical affirmations.

Thanksgiving

My heart rejoices in You, Lord;
My horn is exalted in You.
My mouth boasts over my enemies,
For I delight in Your salvation. (1 Samuel 2:1)

You reached down from on high and took hold of me;
You drew me out of deep waters.
You delivered me from my strong enemy,
From those who hated me,
For they were stronger than I. (2 Samuel 22:17–18)

Pause to offer your own expressions of thanksgiving.

Closing Prayer

Who is like You, O Lord?
Who is like You—majestic in holiness,
Awesome in praises, working wonders? (Exodus 15:11)

There is no one holy like You, O Lord;
There is no one besides You;
Nor is there any Rock like You, our God. (1 Samuel 2:2)

DAY 17

Adoration

> You are the high and lofty One
> Who inhabits eternity, whose name is holy.
> You live in a high and holy place
> But also with the one who is contrite and lowly in spirit.
> You revive the spirit of the lowly
> And the hearts of the contrite. (Isaiah 57:15)

Like the multitudes who went before Jesus, we also shout,

> "Hosanna to the Son of David!
> Blessed is he who comes in the name of the Lord!
> Hosanna in the highest!" (Matthew 21:9)

Pause to express your thoughts of praise and worship.

Confession

> We have sinned with our fathers;
> We have committed iniquity and acted wickedly.
> (Psalm 106:6)

Ask the Spirit to search your heart and reveal any areas of unconfessed sin. Acknowledge these to the Lord and thank Him for His forgiveness.

Renewal

As an obedient child, may I not conform myself to the former lusts I had when I lived in ignorance, but as You who called me are holy, so may I be holy in all my conduct, because it is written: "You shall be holy, for I am holy." (1 Peter 1:14–16)

You are the Lord my God; may I consecrate myself and be holy because You are holy. You are the Lord who brought Your people up out of Egypt to be their God; therefore may I be holy, because You are holy. (Leviticus 11:44–45; 19:2)

Pause to add your own prayers for personal renewal.

Petition

O Lord, I pray, let Your ear be attentive to the prayer of Your servant and to the prayer of Your servants who delight in revering Your name. (Nehemiah 1:11)

Pause here to petition God for spiritual insight so that you might have understanding of His Word. Ask for insight into your identity in Jesus Christ: that you might know who you are, what direction your life should take and what His purpose for your life is. Offer prayers regarding your activities for this day and any special concerns you may have.

Intercession

Lord Jesus, we are encouraged by these words You prayed for all who would believe in You: "I ask that all of them may be one, Father, just as You are in Me and I am in You, that they also may be in Us, that the world may believe that You sent Me. And the glory that You gave Me I have given to them, that they may be one, just as We are one: I in them, and You in Me, that they may be perfected in one, that the world may know that You have sent Me and have loved them, even as You have loved Me." (John 17:21–23)

Take a few moments to intercede on behalf of other believers, such as your personal friends, those in ministry and those who are oppressed and in need.

Affirmation

Father, I rejoice that Your Son Jesus has fulfilled Your promises:

> A Shoot will come forth from the stump of Jesse;
> From his roots a Branch will bear fruit.
> The Spirit of the Lord will rest on Him—
> The Spirit of wisdom and of understanding,
> The Spirit of counsel and of power,
> The Spirit of knowledge and of the fear of the Lord—
> And He will delight in the fear of the Lord.
> He will not judge by what He sees with His eyes,
> Or decide by what He hears with His ears,
> But with righteousness He will judge the poor
> And decide with fairness for the meek of the earth.
> And He will strike the earth with the rod of His mouth;
> With the breath of His lips He will slay the wicked.
> Righteousness will be His belt
> And faithfulness the sash around His waist.
>   (Isaiah 11:1–5)

Behold, a virgin shall be with child and will give birth to a son, and they will call His name Immanuel, which means, "God with us." (Matthew 1:23)

Pause to reflect on these Biblical affirmations.

Thanksgiving

> I cried out, and You heard me
> And saved me out of all my troubles.
> Your angels encamp around those who fear You
> And deliver them. (Psalm 34:6–7)

> I waited patiently for You, Lord,
> And You turned to me and heard my cry.

You lifted me out of the slimy pit, out of the mud and
  mire;
You set my feet on a rock and gave me a firm place to
  stand.
You put a new song in my mouth, a hymn of praise to
  You, my God.
Many will see and fear
And put their trust in You. (Psalm 40:1–3)

Pause to offer your own expressions of thanksgiving.

Closing Prayer

Let the words of my mouth and the meditation of my
  heart
Be pleasing in Your sight,
O Lord, my Rock and my Redeemer. (Psalm 19:14)

Adoration

Blessed are You, O Lord, God of Israel our father, forever and ever. Yours, O Lord, is the greatness and the power and the glory and the victory and the majesty, for everything in heaven and earth is Yours. Yours, O Lord, is the kingdom, and You are exalted as head over all. Both riches and honor come from You, and You are the ruler of all things. In Your hand is power and might to exalt and to give strength to all. Therefore, my God, I give You thanks and I praise Your glorious name. (1 Chronicles 29:10–13)

I will proclaim Your name and praise Your greatness, O God. (Deuteronomy 32:3)

Pause to express your thoughts of praise and worship.

Confession

    O Lord, do not rebuke me in Your wrath,
    And do not chasten me in Your anger.
    For Your arrows have pierced me deeply,
    And Your hand has pressed down upon me.
    There is no health in my body because of Your wrath—
    No peace in my bones because of my sin.
    For my iniquities have gone over my head;
    As a heavy burden, they weigh too much for me.
      (Psalm 38:1–4)

Ask the Spirit to search your heart and reveal any areas of unconfessed sin. Acknowledge these to the Lord and thank Him for His forgiveness.

Renewal

As Your servant, O Christ, and a steward of Your possessions, it is required that I be found faithful. (1 Corinthians 4:1–2)

Those who want to get rich fall into temptation and a snare and into many foolish and harmful desires that plunge them into ruin and destruction. For the love of money is a root of all kinds of evil, and some, by longing for it, have wandered from the faith and pierced themselves with many sorrows. But let me flee from these things and pursue righteousness, godliness, faith, love, patience and gentleness. (1 Timothy 6:9–11)

Pause to add your own prayers for personal renewal.

Petition

May I put away all of these things: anger, wrath, malice, slander and abusive language from my mouth. (Colossians 3:8)

Pause here to petition God for growth in love and compassion toward others. Offer prayers for your loved ones, for those who do not know Jesus and for those in need. Offer prayers regarding your activities for this day and any special concerns you may have.

Intercession

Use me, O God, to open the eyes of others and to turn them from darkness to light, and from the power of Satan to You, so that they may receive forgiveness of sins and an inheritance among those who have been sanctified by faith in Jesus. (Acts 26:18)

Take a few moments to intercede on behalf of friends, relatives, neighbors and coworkers who do not yet know salvation in Jesus Christ.

Affirmation

Blessed are those who persevere under trial, because when they have been approved, they will receive the crown of life that You have promised to those who love You. (James 1:12)

Those who suffer according to Your will should commit themselves to You, their faithful Creator, and continue in doing good. (1 Peter 4:19)

I have overcome, O God, because You are in me, and You are greater than he who is in the world. (1 John 4:4)

Pause to reflect on these Biblical affirmations.

Thanksgiving

My soul blesses You, O Lord;
And all that is within me blesses Your holy name.
My soul blesses You, O Lord,
And I will not forget all Your benefits;
You forgive all my iniquities
And heal all my diseases;
You redeem my life from the pit
And crown me with love and compassion;
You satisfy my desires with good things,
So that my youth is renewed like the eagle's.
(Psalm 103:1–5)

Pause to offer your own expressions of thanksgiving.

Closing Prayer

You, O Lord, are my rock and my fortress and my
    deliverer;
You are my rock; I will take refuge in You.
You are my shield and the horn of my salvation,

My stronghold and my refuge—
My Savior, You save me from violence.
I call on You, Lord; You are worthy of praise,
And I am saved from my enemies. (2 Samuel 22:2–4)

DAY 19

Adoration

How great You are, O Sovereign Lord! There is no one like You, and there is no God besides You, according to all that I have heard with my ears. (2 Samuel 7:22; 1 Chronicles 17:20)

> You alone are the Lord.
> You made the heavens,
> The heaven of heavens, and all their host,
> The earth and all that is on it,
> The seas and all that is in them.
> You give life to all that is in them,
> And the host of heaven worships You. (Nehemiah 9:6)

Pause to express your thoughts of praise and worship.

Confession

Lord, may I learn the importance of forgiveness from Jesus, who was asked by Peter: "Lord, how often shall my brother sin against me, and I forgive him? Up to seven times?" Jesus said to him, "I tell you, not seven times, but up to seventy times seven." (Matthew 18:21–22)

Ask the Spirit to search your heart and reveal any areas of unconfessed sin. Acknowledge these to the Lord and thank Him for His forgiveness.

Renewal

May I not be like those who draw near to You with their mouths and honor You with their lips but whose hearts are far from You; their reverence for You is made up only of rules taught by men. (Isaiah 29:13)

I desire not only to call You "Lord" but to do what You say. By Your grace I will come to You, hear Your words, and put them into practice. Then I will be like someone who built a house, who dug down deep and laid the foundation on rock; when a flood came, the torrent struck that house but could not shake it, because it was well built. (Luke 6:46–48)

Pause to add your own prayers for personal renewal.

Petition

> Guard my soul and rescue me;
> Let me not be ashamed, for I take refuge in You.
> May integrity and uprightness protect me,
> For I wait for You. (Psalm 25:20–21)

Pause here to petition God to help you be a faithful steward of your time, talents, possessions and relationships. Offer prayers of petition regarding your activities for this day and any special concerns you may have.

Intercession

May I submit myself to the governing authorities. For there is no authority except from You, O God, and the authorities that exist have been established by You. Consequently, those who resist authority have opposed Your ordinance, and those who do so will bring judgment on themselves. (Romans 13:1–2)

Take a few moments to intercede on behalf of your local, state or provincial, and national governments. Pray for spiritual revival in the nation and offer prayers regarding current events and concerns.

Affirmation

> Before I was afflicted I went astray,
> But now I keep Your word.

It was good for me to be afflicted,
So that I might learn Your statutes.
I know, O Lord, that Your judgments are righteous,
And that in faithfulness You have afflicted me.
    (Psalm 119:67, 71, 75)

I know that if my earthly house is destroyed, I have a building from You, a house not made with hands, eternal in the heavens. For in this house I groan, longing to be clothed with my heavenly dwelling, because when I am clothed, I will not be found naked. For while I am in this house I groan, being burdened, because I do not want to be unclothed but to be clothed, so that what is mortal may be swallowed up by life. Now You have made me for this very purpose and have given me Your Spirit as a guarantee. (2 Corinthians 5:1–5)

Pause to reflect on these Biblical affirmations.

Thanksgiving

Because You help me,
I will not be disgraced.
Therefore I have set my face like flint,
And I know I will not be put to shame.
You vindicate me, O Lord, and are near;
Who then will contend with me?
Surely You will help me;
Who is he that will condemn me? (Isaiah 50:7–9)

Abba Father, I did not receive a spirit of slavery again to fear, but I received the Spirit of adoption by whom I cry to You. The Spirit Himself testifies with my spirit that I am Your child. (Romans 8:15–16)

Pause to offer your own expressions of thanksgiving.

Closing Prayer

Lord Jesus, all those the Father gives You will come to You, and whoever comes to You, You will never cast out. For You have come down from heaven, not to do Your own will, but the will of Him who sent You. And this is the will of Him who sent You, that You will lose none of all that He has given You, but raise them up at the last day. For Your Father's will is that those who look to You and believe in You may have eternal life, and You will raise them up at the last day. (John 6:37–40)

Adoration

> We praise You, Lord!
> We praise You in Your sanctuary;
> We praise You in Your mighty heavens.
> We praise You for Your mighty acts;
> We praise You according to Your excellent greatness.
> We praise You with the sound of the trumpet;
> We praise You with the harp and lyre.
> We praise You with the timbrel and dancing;
> We praise You with stringed instruments and flutes.
> We praise You on the sounding cymbals;
> We praise You on the resounding cymbals.
> Let everything that has breath praise You.
> We praise You, Lord! (Psalm 150:1–6)

You, O Lord, shall reign for ever and ever. (Exodus 15:18)

Pause to express your thoughts of praise and worship.

Confession

> Heal me, O Lord, and I will be healed;
> Save me, and I will be saved,
> For You are the One I praise. (Jeremiah 17:14)

Ask the Spirit to search your heart and reveal any areas of unconfessed sin. Acknowledge these to the Lord and thank Him for His forgiveness.

Renewal

Since I call on You, Father, who judge each person's work impartially, may I conduct myself in fear during the time of my sojourn on earth. (1 Peter 1:17)

May I keep Your commandments, O Lord my God, and walk in Your ways and fear You. May I follow You and fear You; may I keep Your commandments, hear Your voice, serve You and hold fast to You. (Deuteronomy 8:6; 13:4)

Pause to add your own prayers for personal renewal.

Petition

Lord, help me to be careful and watch myself closely, lest I forget the things my eyes have seen or let them depart from my heart as long as I live. May I teach them to my children and to their children after them. (Deuteronomy 4:9)

Pause here to offer prayers of petition regarding your family and your ministry. Ask for help and guidance in sharing Jesus with others and helping others grow in Him. Ask for guidance in your vocation and your avocations. Offer prayers of petition regarding your activities for this day and any special concerns you may have.

Intercession

With all prayer and petition, we should pray always in Your Spirit, and to this end we should be watchful with all perseverance and petition for all the saints. (Ephesians 6:18)

Take a few moments to intercede on behalf of local, national and world missions. Pray that the Great Commission would be fulfilled and for any special concerns you may have for missions.

Affirmation

Lord, You have told us: "Many who are first will be last, and the last will be first." (Matthew 19:30; Mark 10:31)

Those who wish to become great among others must become their servant, and those who wish to be first among them must be their slave. (Matthew 20:26–27; Mark 10:43–44)

Those who exalt themselves will be humbled, and those who humble themselves will be exalted. (Matthew 23:12; Luke 14:11; 18:14)

Pause to reflect on these Biblical affirmations.

Thanksgiving

> The heavens shout for joy! The earth rejoices!
> The mountains break out into singing!
> For You have comforted Your people
> And will have compassion on Your afflicted ones.
>   (Isaiah 49:13)

> I will greatly rejoice in You, O Lord;
> My soul will be joyful in You, my God.
> For You have clothed me with garments of salvation
> And arrayed me in a robe of righteousness,
> As a bridegroom decks himself with ornaments,
> And as a bride adorns herself with her jewels.
>   (Isaiah 61:10)

Pause to offer your own expressions of thanksgiving.

Closing Prayer

> You will command Your lovingkindness by day,
> In the night Your song is with me—
> A prayer to You, the God of my life. (Psalm 42:8)

> Blessed are You, Lord God, the God of Israel,
> Who alone does wonderful things.
> Blessed be Your glorious name forever;
> May the whole earth be filled with Your glory.
> Amen and Amen. (Psalm 72:18–19)

DAY 21

Adoration

O God, in the year that King Uzziah died, Isaiah saw You sitting on a throne, high and exalted, and the train of Your robe filled the temple. Above it stood the seraphim; each one had six wings: with two they covered their faces, with two they covered their feet, and with two they flew. And one cried to the other and said, "Holy, Holy, Holy is the Lord of hosts; the whole earth is full of His glory!" (Isaiah 6:1–3)

You, Lord God, are the Alpha and the Omega. You are the One who is, and who was, and who is to come, the Almighty. (Revelation 1:8)

Pause to express your thoughts of praise and worship.

Confession

For You, the Lord God, have said,
"I, even I, am He who blots out your transgressions for
    My own sake,
And I will not remember your sins." (Isaiah 43:25)

Ask the Spirit to search your heart and reveal any areas of unconfessed sin. Acknowledge these to the Lord and thank Him for His forgiveness.

Renewal

Lord, You have taught us: "You shall love the Lord your God with all your heart and with all your soul and with all your mind." This is the first and greatest commandment. And the second is like it: "You shall love your neighbor as yourself." All the Law and the Prophets hang on these two commandments. (Matthew 22:37–40)

May I not love with words or tongue, but in deed and in truth. By this I will know that I am of the truth and my heart will be assured before You, O God; for if my heart condemns me, You are greater than my heart, and You know all things. If my heart does not condemn me, I have confidence before You and receive from You whatever I ask, because I keep Your commandments and do the things that are pleasing in Your sight. (1 John 3:18–22)

Pause to add your own prayers for personal renewal.

Petition

May I not say, "Today or tomorrow I will go to this or that city, spend a year there, carry on business, and make a profit." For I do not even know what my life will be tomorrow. I am a vapor that appears for a little while and then vanishes away. Instead, let me say, "If the Lord wills, I will live and do this or that." Otherwise, I boast in my arrogance, and all such boasting is evil. (James 4:13–16)

Pause here to petition God for growth in your character and personal discipline, and for physical health and strength. Ask that He empower you for spiritual warfare against the temptations of the world, the flesh and the devil. Offer prayers regarding your activities for this day and any special concerns you may have.

Intercession

May I remember those in prison as though bound with them, and those who are mistreated, as though suffering with them. (Hebrews 13:3)

Take a few moments to intercede on behalf of the poor and hungry, the oppressed and persecuted, and those in control of world and national resources. Offer prayers for peace among nations and regarding current events and concerns.

Affirmation

O God, apart from the law, Your righteousness has been made known, being witnessed by the Law and the Prophets, even Your righteousness through faith in Jesus Christ to all who believe. For there is no difference, for all have sinned and fall short of Your glory, being justified freely by Your grace through the redemption that is in Christ Jesus. (Romans 3:21–24)

What the law was powerless to do, in that it was weakened through the flesh, You did by sending Your own Son in the likeness of sinful flesh, on account of sin; You condemned sin in the flesh, in order that the requirement of the law might be fully met in us, who do not walk according to the flesh, but according to Your Spirit. (Romans 8:3–4)

Pause to reflect on these Biblical affirmations.

Thanksgiving

For those who revere Your name, the sun of righteousness will rise with healing in his wings. And they will go out and leap like calves released from the stall. (Malachi 4:2)

> Lord Jesus, we rejoice that you fulfilled the words of the prophet Isaiah:
>
> "The Spirit of the Lord is upon Me,
> Because He has anointed Me to preach good news to the poor.
> He has sent Me to proclaim freedom for the captives
> And recovery of sight to the blind,
> To set free those who are downtrodden,
> To proclaim the acceptable year of the Lord."
> (Luke 4:18–19)

Pause to offer your own expressions of thanksgiving.

Closing Prayer

I will enter Your gates with thanksgiving
And Your courts with praise;
I will give thanks to You and bless Your name.
For You are good
And Your lovingkindness endures forever;
Your faithfulness continues through all generations.
(Psalm 100:4–5)

May Your glory endure forever;
May You rejoice in Your works. (Psalm 104:31)

DAY 22

Adoration

A great multitude, which no one could number, from all nations and tribes and peoples and languages will stand before the throne and before the Lamb, clothed with white robes, with palm branches in their hands, and will cry out with a loud voice, "Salvation belongs to You, our God, who sits on the throne, and to the Lamb!" (Revelation 7:9–10)

Blessed are You, Jesus, the King who comes in the name of the Lord!
Peace in heaven and glory in the highest! (Luke 19:38)

Pause to express your thoughts of praise and worship.

Confession

Your eyes are everywhere, O Lord,
Keeping watch on the evil and the good. (Proverbs 15:3)

Ask the Spirit to search your heart and reveal any areas of unconfessed sin. Acknowledge these to the Lord and thank Him for His forgiveness.

Renewal

Like Abraham, may I call upon Your name; You are the Everlasting God. (Genesis 13:4; 21:33)

May I listen carefully to Your voice, Lord God, and do what is right in Your sight; may I pay attention to Your commandments and keep all Your statutes. (Exodus 15:26)

May I rejoice in my tribulations, knowing that tribulation produces perseverance; and perseverance, character; and character, hope. And hope does not disappoint, because Your love, O God, has been poured out into my heart through the Holy Spirit, whom You have given to me. (Romans 5:3–5)

Pause to add your own prayers for personal renewal.

Petition

> May Your merciful kindness be my comfort,
> According to Your promise to Your servant.
>   (Psalm 119:76)

Pause here to petition God for growth in your desire to know and please Jesus Christ. Pray for a greater love and commitment to Him, for the grace to practice His presence and for the grace to glorify Him in your life. Offer prayers regarding your activities for this day and any special concerns you may have.

Intercession

> Is this not the fast You have chosen:
> To loose the bonds of wickedness,
> To undo the cords of the yoke,
> And to let the oppressed go free
> And break every yoke?
> Is it not to share our food with the hungry
> And to provide the poor wanderer with shelter;
> When we see the naked, to clothe them,
> And not to turn away from our own flesh?
> Then our light will break forth like the dawn,
> And our healing will quickly appear,
> And our righteousness will go before us;
> Your glory, O Lord, will be our rear guard.
> Then we will call, and You will answer;
> We will cry, and You will say, "Here I am."
> If we put away the yoke from our midst,

The pointing of the finger and malicious talk,
And if we extend our souls to the hungry
And satisfy the afflicted soul,
Then our light will rise in the darkness,
And our gloom will become like the noonday.
   (Isaiah 58:6–10)

Take a few moments to intercede on behalf of your local church, other churches, evangelism and discipleship ministries, educational ministries and any other special concerns you may have.

Affirmation

By Your will, my God, I have been sanctified through the offering of the body of Jesus Christ once for all. And every priest stands daily ministering and offering again and again the same sacrifices, which can never take away sins. But when this Priest had offered for all time one sacrifice for sins, He sat down at Your right hand, waiting from that time for His enemies to be made a footstool for His feet. For by one offering He has made perfect forever those who are being sanctified. (Hebrews 10:10–14)

Lord Jesus Christ, I acknowledge that you suffered for me, leaving me an example that I should follow in Your steps. For "[You] committed no sin, and no deceit was found in [Your] mouth." When You were reviled, You did not retaliate; when You suffered, You made no threats, but entrusted Yourself to God who judges righteously; and You Yourself bore our sins in Your body on the tree, so that I might die to sins and live for righteousness; by Your wounds I have been healed. For I was like a sheep going astray, but now I have returned to You, the Shepherd and Overseer of my soul. (1 Peter 2:21–25)

Pause to reflect on these Biblical affirmations.

Thanksgiving

From Your fullness, O Christ, we have all received grace upon grace. For the law was given through Moses; grace and truth came through You. (John 1:16–17)

Jesus, You are the Lamb of God, who takes away the sin of the world. (John 1:29)

Pause to offer your own expressions of thanksgiving.

Closing Prayer

You, O Lord, will keep me from all evil;
You will preserve my soul.
You will watch over my coming and going
From this time forth and forever. (Psalm 121:7–8)

DAY 23

Adoration

You are great and most worthy of praise, O Lord;
You are to be feared above all gods.
For all the gods of the nations are idols,
But You made the heavens.
Splendor and majesty are before You;
Strength and beauty are in Your sanctuary.
I will ascribe to You glory and strength.
I will ascribe to You the glory due Your name
And worship You in the beauty of holiness.
   (Psalm 96:4–9)

Blessed is the one who fears You,
Who finds great delight in Your commands.
   (Psalm 112:1)

Pause to express your thoughts of praise and worship.

Confession

I confess my iniquity;
I am troubled by my sin.
O Lord, do not forsake me;
O my God, be not far from me!
Make haste to help me,
O Lord my salvation. (Psalm 38:18, 21–22)

*Ask the Spirit to search your heart and reveal any areas of
unconfessed sin. Acknowledge these to the Lord and thank Him
for His forgiveness.*

Renewal

May I be faithful and fear You, O God. (Nehemiah 7:2)

O God, I have this hope in You: that there will be a resurrection of both the righteous and the wicked. In view of this, may I strive always to keep my conscience blameless before You and before all people. (Acts 24:15–16)

Pause to add your own prayers for personal renewal.

Petition

May I not take revenge, but leave room for Your wrath, O God, for You have said, "Vengeance is Mine; I will repay." May I not be overcome by evil, but overcome evil with good. (Deuteronomy 32:35; Romans 12:19, 21)

Pause here to petition God for wisdom. Ask Him to develop your eternal perspective, to renew your mind with truth and to help you develop greater skill in each area of your life. Offer prayers regarding your activities for this day and any special concerns you may have.

Intercession

May Your commandments be upon my heart, so that I may teach them diligently to my children and talk about them when I sit in my house and when I walk along the way and when I lie down and when I rise up. (Deuteronomy 6:6–7)

Take a few moments to intercede on behalf of your immediate family and other relatives. Offer prayers for their spiritual, emotional and physical concerns.

Affirmation

Jesus, You are the way and the truth and the life. No one comes to the Father except through You. (John 14:6)

Lord Jesus, through You the forgiveness of sins is proclaimed: Through You everyone who believes is justified from all

things from which they could not be justified by the law of
Moses. (Acts 13:38–39)

Through faith I am guarded by Your power, O God, for the
salvation that is ready to be revealed in the last time. (1 Peter
1:5)

Pause to reflect on these Biblical affirmations.

Thanksgiving

Lord Jesus, You were oppressed and afflicted,
Yet You did not open Your mouth;
You were led like a lamb to the slaughter,
And as a sheep before her shearers is silent,
So You did not open Your mouth.
By oppression and judgment You were taken away.
And who can speak of Your descendants?
For You were cut off from the land of the living;
You were stricken for the transgression of God's people.
You were assigned a grave with the wicked,
Yet with a rich man in Your death,
Though You had done no violence,
Nor was any deceit in Your mouth.
Yet it was the Lord's will
To crush You and cause You to suffer.
Though the Lord made You a guilt offering,
You will see Your offspring and prolong Your days,
And the pleasure of the Lord will prosper in Your hand.
You will see the fruit of the travail of Your soul and be
    satisfied;
You who are God's righteous servant will justify many
    by Your knowledge.
And You will bear their iniquities.
Therefore, God will give You a portion among the great,
And You will divide the spoils with the strong,

Because You poured out Your life unto death,
And were numbered with the transgressors.
For You bore the sin of many,
And made intercession for the transgressors.
   (Isaiah 53:7–12)

Pause to offer your own expressions of thanksgiving.

Closing Prayer

I will trust in You, O Lord,
And lean not on my own understanding;
In all my ways I will acknowledge You,
And You will make my paths straight.
I will not be wise in my own eyes,
But fear You and depart from evil. (Proverbs 3:5–7)

DAY 24

Adoration

O Son of Man, You will come with the clouds of heaven. In the presence of the Ancient of Days, You will be given dominion and glory and a kingdom, so that people of every nation and language will worship You. Your dominion is an everlasting dominion that will not pass away, and Your kingdom is one that will never be destroyed. (Daniel 7:13–14)

Jesus, You are my Lord and my God. (John 20:28)

Pause to express your thoughts of praise and worship.

Confession

Who may ascend Your holy hill, O Lord?
Who may stand in Your holy place?
Those who have clean hands and pure hearts,
Who have not lifted up their souls to idols
Or sworn by what is false. (Psalm 24:3–4)

Ask the Spirit to search your heart and reveal any areas of unconfessed sin. Acknowledge these to the Lord and thank Him for His forgiveness.

Renewal

O Lord my God, may You be with me as You were with our fathers; may You never leave me nor forsake me. Incline my heart to You, that I may walk in all Your ways and keep Your commands and Your statutes and Your judgments, which You gave our fathers. May all the peoples of the earth know that You, Lord, are God; there is no other. Let my heart be fully committed to You, the Lord my God, to walk in Your statutes and keep Your commandments, as at this day. (1 Kings 8:57–58, 60–61)

As one who knows righteousness, who has Your law in my heart, may I not fear the reproach of others or be terrified by their revilings. (Isaiah 51:7)

Pause to add your own prayers for personal renewal.

Petition

Lord, may I learn the divine perspective Joseph had when he said to his brothers, "Do not be grieved or angry with yourselves for selling me here, for God sent me before you to save lives. He sent me ahead of you to preserve for you a remnant on earth and to save your lives by a great deliverance. So it was not you who sent me here, but God." (Genesis 45:5, 7–8)

Pause here to petition God for spiritual insight so that you might have understanding of His Word. Ask for insight into your identity in Jesus Christ: that you might know who you are, what direction your life should take and what His purpose for your life is. Offer prayers regarding your activities for this day and any special concerns you may have.

Intercession

May we be deeply devoted to one another, honoring one another above ourselves. (Romans 12:10)

Take a few moments to intercede on behalf of other believers, such as your personal friends, those in ministry and those who are oppressed and in need.

Affirmation

Jesus taught that I cannot serve two masters; I will hate the one and love the other, or I will be devoted to the one and despise the other. Therefore, I know I cannot serve both You, O God, and wealth. (Matthew 6:24; Luke 16:13)

If I am rich in this present world, I should not be arrogant or set my hope on the uncertainty of riches but on You, O God, for You richly provide me with everything for my enjoyment. I should do good, be rich in good works, and be generous and willing to share. In this way, I will lay up treasure for myself as a firm foundation for the future, so that I may lay hold of true life. (1 Timothy 6:17–19)

Pause to reflect on these Biblical affirmations.

Thanksgiving

I will sing to You, O Lord, and give praise to You,
For You have rescued the lives of the needy
From the hands of evildoers. (Jeremiah 20:13)

You, O Lord, are good,
A refuge in times of trouble;
You know those who trust in You. (Nahum 1:7)

Pause to offer your own expressions of thanksgiving.

Closing Prayer

You, O Lord, have said: "Let not those who are wise boast of their wisdom, and let not those who are strong boast of their strength, and let not those who are rich boast of their riches; but let those who boast, boast about this: that they understand and know Me, that I am the Lord, who exercises lovingkindness, justice and righteousness on earth; in these I delight." (Jeremiah 9:23–24)

"You are my portion, Lord," says my soul;
Therefore I will wait for You.
You are good to those who wait for You,
To the soul who seeks You.
It is good to hope silently
For Your salvation. (Lamentations 3:24–26)

DAY 25

Adoration

You, Almighty Creator, asked:
"Where were you when I laid the foundations of the
    earth?
Tell Me, if you have understanding.
Who determined its measurements?
Surely you know!
Or who stretched the line across it?
On what were its bases sunk,
Or who laid its cornerstone
When the morning stars sang together
And all the children of God shouted for joy?"
    (Job 38:4–7)

You revealed Yourself to Moses as "I AM WHO I AM."
    (Exodus 3:14)

Pause to express your thoughts of praise and worship.

Confession

You have been just in all that has happened to me, O God;
You have acted faithfully, while I did wrong. (Nehemiah 9:33)

*Ask the Spirit to search your heart and reveal any areas of
unconfessed sin. Acknowledge these to the Lord and thank Him
for His forgiveness.*

Renewal

Jesus, if I abide in You, and Your words abide in me, I can ask
whatever I wish, and it will be done for me. As I ask in Your
name, I will receive, that my joy may be full. (John 15:7, 16:24)

As I walk in Your Spirit, I will not fulfill the desires of the flesh. For the flesh desires what is contrary to the Spirit, and the Spirit what is contrary to the flesh; for they oppose each other, so that I may not do the things that I wish. But if I am led by Your Spirit, I am not under the law. (Galatians 5:16–18)

Pause to add your own prayers for personal renewal.

Petition

May I be above reproach, temperate, sensible, respectable, hospitable, able to teach, not given to drunkenness, not violent but gentle, not quarrelsome, not a lover of money, one who manages my own family well, and who keeps my children under control with proper respect. Grant me a good reputation with outsiders, so that I will not fall into disgrace and the snare of the devil. (1 Timothy 3:2–4, 7)

Pause here to petition God for growth in love and compassion toward others. Offer prayers for your loved ones, for those who do not know Jesus and for those in need. Offer prayers regarding your activities for this day and any special concerns you may have.

Intercession

Because I know what it means to fear You, Lord, may I seek to persuade other people. (2 Corinthians 5:11)

Take a few moments to intercede on behalf of friends, relatives, neighbors and coworkers who do not yet know salvation in Jesus Christ.

Affirmation

You are righteous; You love righteousness;
The upright will see Your face. (Psalm 11:7)

Lord, who may dwell in Your tabernacle?
Who may live on Your holy mountain?
Those who walk uprightly and work righteousness
And speak the truth in their hearts;
They neither slander with their tongues
Nor do evil to their neighbors
Nor take up a reproach against their friends;
They despise the reprobate
But honor those who fear You.
They keep their oath even when it hurts,
Lend their money without interest,
And do not accept bribes against the innocent.
Those who do these things will never be shaken.
    (Psalm 15:1–5)

Pause to reflect on these Biblical affirmations.

Thanksgiving

Lord, You completed the heavens and the earth in all their vast array. By the seventh day You finished the work that You had done, and rested on the seventh day from all Your creative work. (Genesis 2:1–2)

Lord God, You formed a man from the dust of the ground and breathed into his nostrils the breath of life; and he became a living being. (Genesis 2:7)

Pause to offer your own expressions of thanksgiving.

Closing Prayer

Who shall separate me from Your love, O Christ? Shall tribulation, or distress, or persecution, or famine, or nakedness, or danger, or sword? As it is written: "For Your sake we face death all day long; we are considered as sheep to be slaughtered." Yet in all these things I am more than a conqueror through You, the One who loved me. (Romans 8:35–37)

DAY 26

Adoration

> You are the living God,
> And there is no god besides You.
> You put to death and You bring to life,
> You have wounded and You will heal,
> And no one can deliver from Your hand.
> (Deuteronomy 32:39)

> I will remember the former things, those of long ago;
> You are God, and there is no other;
> You are God, and there is none like You. (Isaiah 46:9)

Pause to express your thoughts of praise and worship.

Confession

When I sin against You, Lord, I may be sure that my sin will find me out. (Numbers 32:23)

Ask the Spirit to search your heart and reveal any areas of unconfessed sin. Acknowledge these to the Lord and thank Him for His forgiveness.

Renewal

May I not be conformed to the pattern of this world but be transformed by the renewing of my mind, that I may be able to test and approve that Your will is good and pleasing and perfect. (Romans 12:2)

O God of my Lord Jesus Christ, the Father of glory, may You give me a spirit of wisdom and of revelation in the full knowledge of You, and may the eyes of my heart be enlightened, in order that I may know what is the hope of Your calling, what are the riches of Your glorious inheritance in the saints, and what is the incomparable greatness of Your power toward us who believe. (Ephesians 1:17–19)

Pause to add your own prayers for personal renewal.

Petition

Whatever I do, may I do it all to Your glory, O God. (1 Corinthians 10:31)

Pause here to petition God to help you be a faithful steward of your time, talents, possessions and relationships. Offer prayers of petition regarding your activities for this day and any special concerns you may have.

Intercession

May we offer petitions, prayers, intercessions and thanksgivings on behalf of all people, for kings and all those who are in authority, that we may live peaceful and quiet lives in all godliness and reverence. This is good and acceptable in Your sight, God our Savior, for You desire all people to be saved and to come to the knowledge of the truth. (1 Timothy 2:1–4)

Take a few moments to intercede on behalf of your local, state or provincial, and national governments. Pray for spiritual revival in the nation and offer prayers regarding current events and concerns.

Affirmation

There is a time for everything, and a season for every activity under heaven. (Ecclesiastes 3:1)

O God, You have made everything beautiful in its time. You have also set eternity in human hearts; yet they cannot fathom what You have done from beginning to end. (Ecclesiastes 3:11)

Pause to reflect on these Biblical affirmations.

Thanksgiving

I do not lose heart; even though my outward self is perishing, yet my inner self is being renewed day by day. For this light affliction, which is momentary, is working for me a far more exceeding and eternal weight of glory. So I do not look at the things that are seen but at the things that are unseen. For the things which are seen are temporary, but the things that are unseen are eternal. (2 Corinthians 4:16–18)

Pause to offer your own expressions of thanksgiving.

Closing Prayer

May we glory in Your holy name, O Lord.
Let the hearts of those who seek You rejoice.
May we seek You and Your strength;
May we seek Your face always.
May we remember the wonderful works You have done,
Your miracles and the judgments You pronounced.
(1 Chronicles 16:10–12)

O Lord, You reign forever;
You have established Your throne for judgment.
You will judge the world in righteousness,
And You will govern the peoples with justice.
You will also be a refuge for the oppressed,
A stronghold in times of trouble.
Those who know Your name will trust in You,
For You, Lord, have never forsaken those who seek You.
(Psalm 9:7–10)

Adoration

> We praise You, Lord!
> All Your servants praise You;
> We praise Your name, O Lord.
> Blessed be Your name
> Both now and forever.
> From the rising of the sun to its setting,
> Your name, O Lord, is to be praised.
> You are high above all nations,
> Your glory above the heavens.
> Who is like You, O Lord our God,
> The One who is enthroned on high,
> Who humbles Himself to behold
> The things that are in the heavens and in the earth?
> (Psalm 113:1–6)

Pause to express your thoughts of praise and worship.

Confession

> You, the Lord our Redeemer, have said,
> "For a brief moment I forsook you,
> But with great compassion I will gather you.
> In a flood of anger I hid My face from you for a moment,
> But I will have compassion on you with everlasting
> kindness." (Isaiah 54:7–8)

Ask the Spirit to search your heart and reveal any areas of unconfessed sin. Acknowledge these to the Lord and thank Him for His forgiveness.

Renewal

Like Job, may I be blameless and upright, fearing You and shunning evil. (Job 1:1)

May I be careful to lead a blameless life.
May I walk in the integrity of my heart in the midst of
    my house.
May I set no wicked thing before my eyes.
I hate the deeds of those who fall away;
May their deeds not cling to me. (Psalm 101:2–3)

Pause to add your own prayers for personal renewal.

Petition

Even when I am old and gray, do not forsake me, O God,
Until I declare Your strength to the next generation,
Your power to all who are to come. (Psalm 71:18)

*Pause here to offer prayers of petition regarding your family and
your ministry. Ask for help and guidance in sharing Jesus with
others and helping others grow in Him. Ask for guidance in your
vocation and your avocations. Offer prayers of petition regarding your activities for this day and any special concerns you may
have.*

Intercession

O God, be gracious to us and bless us,
And make Your face shine upon us,
That Your way may be known on earth,
Your salvation among all nations. (Psalm 67:1–2)

*Take a few moments to intercede on behalf of local, national
and world missions. Pray that the Great Commission would be
fulfilled and for any special concerns you may have for missions.*

Affirmation

The wolf will dwell with the lamb,
And the leopard will lie down with the goat,
And the calf and the lion and the yearling together,

And a little child will lead them.
The cow will feed with the bear;
Their young will lie down together,
And the lion will eat straw like the ox.
The infant will play near the hole of the cobra,
And the young child will put his hand into the viper's
    hole.
They will neither harm nor destroy on all Your holy
    mountain,
For the earth will be full of Your knowledge, O Lord.
As the waters cover the sea. (Isaiah 11:6–9)

As the earth brings forth its sprouts
And as a garden causes that which is sown to spring up,
So You, Lord God, will make righteousness
And praise spring up before all nations. (Isaiah 61:11)

Pause to reflect on these Biblical affirmations.

Thanksgiving

By grace I have been saved through faith, and this not of
myself; it is Your gift to me, and not of works, so that I cannot boast. (Ephesians 2:8–9)

I am confident of this, that You, the One who began a good
work in me, will carry it on to completion until the day of
Christ Jesus. (Philippians 1:6)

Pause to offer your own expressions of thanksgiving.

Closing Prayer

Blessed are those who have learned to acclaim You,
Who walk in the light of Your presence, O Lord.
They rejoice in Your name all day long,
And they exult in Your righteousness. (Psalm 89:15–16)

DAY 28

Adoration

> You have measured the waters in the hollow of Your
>   hand,
> And marked off the heavens with the breadth of Your
>   hand.
> You have calculated the dust of the earth in a measure,
> And weighed the mountains in the balance
> And the hills in scales. (Isaiah 40:12)
>
> You are the Lord, and there is no other;
> Apart from You there is no God.
> From the rising of the sun to its setting,
> We know there is none besides You.
> You are the Lord, and there is no other. (Isaiah 45:5–6)

Pause to express your thoughts of praise and worship.

Confession

> When my soul was fainting away,
> I remembered You, Lord,
> And my prayer went up to You—to Your holy temple.
> Those who cling to worthless idols
> Forsake Your lovingkindness.
> But I will sacrifice to You
> With the voice of thanksgiving.
> I will fulfill what I have vowed.
> Salvation is from You alone. (Jonah 2:7–9)

*Ask the Spirit to search your heart and reveal any areas of
unconfessed sin. Acknowledge these to the Lord and thank Him
for His forgiveness.*

Renewal

I am the salt of the earth. But if the salt loses its flavor, how can it be made salty again? It is no longer good for anything, except to be thrown out and trampled underfoot by people. I am the light of the world. A city set on a hill cannot be hidden. Neither do people light a lamp and put it under a basket, but on a lampstand, and it gives light to all who are in the house. In the same way, I must let my light shine before all people, that they may see my good deeds and praise You, my Father in heaven. (Matthew 5:13–16)

I want to walk in a way that is worthy of the calling I have received, with all humility and meekness and patience. (Ephesians 4:1–2)

Pause to add your own prayers for personal renewal.

Petition

May I be strong and courageous; may I not be afraid or discouraged, for You, Lord my God, will be with me wherever I go. (Joshua 1:9)

Pause here to petition God for growth in your character and personal discipline, and for physical health and strength. Ask that He empower you for spiritual warfare against the temptations of the world, the flesh and the devil. Offer prayers regarding your activities for this day and any special concerns you may have.

Intercession

O Lord, the great and awesome God, You are the One who keeps Your covenant and lovingkindness with those who love You and with those who obey Your commandments. We have sinned and committed iniquity; we have been wicked and have rebelled, even turning away from Your commandments and from Your judgments. To You alone belong mercy and forgiveness, even though we have rebelled against You. We have not obeyed Your voice to walk in Your laws, which You set before us through Your servants the prophets. (Daniel 9:4–5, 9–10)

Take a few moments to intercede on behalf of the poor and hungry, the oppressed and persecuted, and those in control of world and national resources. Offer prayers for peace among nations and regarding current events and concerns.

Affirmation

Cursed are those who trust in people,
Who depend on flesh for their strength
And whose hearts turn away from You, Lord.
But blessed are those who trust in You,
Whose confidence is in You. (Jeremiah 17:5, 7)

Jesus, You knew all people, and had no need for anyone's testimony about them, for You knew what was in them. (John 2:24–25)

O God, You will judge the secrets of all people through Jesus Christ, according to the gospel. (Romans 2:16)

Pause to reflect on these Biblical affirmations.

Thanksgiving

May I rejoice in You always, O Lord. (Philippians 4:4)

You, O God my Savior, have called me, and Christ Jesus is my hope. (1 Timothy 1:1)

Pause to offer your own expressions of thanksgiving.

Closing Prayer

We praise You, O Lord!
We praise You from the heavens;

We praise You in the heights.
You are praised by all Your angels;
You are praised by all Your heavenly hosts.
The sun and moon praise You;
All the shining stars praise You;
The highest heavens praise You
And the waters above the heavens.
Everything praises Your name, O Lord,
For You commanded and they were created.
You established them for ever and ever;
You gave a decree that will not pass away.
   (Psalm 148:1–6)

DAY 29

Adoration

May I enter into the adoration John witnessed when he heard the voice of many angels encircling the throne and the living creatures and the elders; and their number was myriads of myriads, and thousands of thousands, saying with a loud voice:

"Worthy are You, the Lamb who was slain,
To receive power and riches and wisdom
And strength and honor and glory and blessing!"
(Revelation 5:11–12)

You, Lord Jesus Christ, received honor and glory from God the Father when the voice came to You from the Majestic Glory, saying, "This is My beloved Son, with whom I am well pleased." (2 Peter 1:17)

Pause to express your thoughts of praise and worship.

Confession

I will not forget the exhortation that addresses me as Your child:

"My child, do not despise the Lord's discipline,
Nor lose heart when you are rebuked by Him,
For whom the Lord loves He disciplines,
And He chastises every child whom He receives."
(Hebrews 12:5–6)

Ask the Spirit to search your heart and reveal any areas of unconfessed sin. Acknowledge these to the Lord and thank Him for His forgiveness.

Renewal

May I fear You and keep Your commandments, for this applies to every person. (Ecclesiastes 12:13)

> Give me understanding, and I will keep Your law
> And observe it with all my heart.
> Make me walk in the path of Your commands,
> For there I find delight.
> Incline my heart to Your testimonies
> And not to selfish gain.
> Turn my eyes away from worthless things,
> And revive me in Your way. (Psalm 119:34–37)

Pause to add your own prayers for personal renewal.

Petition

Like Ezra, I want to set my heart to study Your Word, to obey it and to do it, and to teach it to others. (Ezra 7:10)

Pause here to petition God for growth in your desire to know and please Jesus Christ. Pray for a greater love and commitment to Him, for the grace to practice His presence and for the grace to glorify Him in your life. Offer prayers regarding your activities for this day and any special concerns you may have.

Intercession

Since we were called into fellowship with You, Lord Jesus Christ, help us to agree with one another, so that there may be no divisions among us, and that we may be perfectly joined together in the same mind and in the same judgment. (1 Corinthians 1:9–10)

Take a few moments to intercede on behalf of your local church, other churches, evangelism and discipleship ministries, educational ministries and any other special concerns you may have.

Affirmation

I will not lay up for myself treasures on earth, where moth
and rust destroy and where thieves break in and steal. But I
will lay up for myself treasures in heaven, where moth and
rust do not destroy and where thieves do not break in and
steal. For where my treasure is, there my heart will be also.
(Matthew 6:19–21; Luke 12:34)

O God, Your divine power has given me all things that per-
tain to life and godliness through my knowledge of You who
called me by Your own glory and virtue. Through these You
have given me Your very great and precious promises, so that
through them I may be a partaker of the divine nature, having escaped the corruption that is in the world by lust.
(2 Peter 1:3–4)

Pause to reflect on these Biblical affirmations.

Thanksgiving

Surely Your hand is not too short to save,
Nor Your ear too dull to hear.
But our iniquities have separated us from You, our
    God;
Our sins have hidden Your face from us, so that You
    will not hear.
Yet You saw that there was no one to intervene;
So Your own arm worked salvation for You,
And Your righteousness sustained You.
You put on righteousness as Your breastplate,
And the helmet of salvation on Your head;
You put on the garments of vengeance
And wrapped Yourself in zeal as a cloak.
From the west, all people will fear Your name,
And from the rising of the sun, they will revere Your
    glory.

For You will come like a flood
That Your breath drives along. (Isaiah 59:1–2, 16–19)

Pause to offer your own expressions of thanksgiving.

Closing Prayer

O God, I am convinced that neither death nor life, nor
angels nor principalities, nor things present nor things to
come, nor powers, nor height nor depth, nor anything else
in all creation will be able to separate me from Your love that
is in Christ Jesus my Lord. (Romans 8:38–39)

DAY 30

Adoration

May I fear You, the Lord my God; may I serve You, hold fast to You, and take my oaths in Your name. For You are my praise and You are my God, who performed for me these great and awesome wonders, which I have seen with my own eyes. (Deuteronomy 10:20–21)

You are the great, the mighty, and the awesome God, who keeps Your covenant of lovingkindness. (Nehemiah 9:32)

Pause to express your thoughts of praise and worship.

Confession

From within, out of our hearts, proceed evil thoughts, sexual immorality, thefts, murders, adulteries, greed, wickedness, deceit, lewdness, envy, slander, arrogance and folly. All these evil things come from within our hearts and defile us. (Mark 7:21–23)

Ask the Spirit to search your heart and reveal any areas of unconfessed sin. Acknowledge these to the Lord and thank Him for His forgiveness.

Renewal

I will not let sin reign in my mortal body that I should obey its evil desires. Nor will I present the parts of my body to sin as instruments of wickedness, but I will present myself to You, Lord God, as one who is alive from the dead. I will present the parts of my body as instruments of righteousness to You. (Romans 6:12–13)

May I put away all filthiness and the overflow of wickedness, and in meekness accept the word planted in me, which is able to save my soul. (James 1:21)

Pause to add your own prayers for personal renewal.

Petition

I call on You, O God, for You will answer me;
Incline Your ear to me and hear my prayer.
Show Your wonderful lovingkindness,
O Savior of those who take refuge at Your right hand
From those who rise up against them.
Keep me as the apple of Your eye;
Hide me in the shadow of Your wings. (Psalm 17:6–8)

Pause here to petition God for wisdom. Ask Him to develop your eternal perspective, to renew your mind with truth and to help you develop greater skill in each area of your life. Offer prayers regarding your activities for this day and any special concerns you may have.

Intercession

I am not to seek my own good, but rather the good of others. (1 Corinthians 10:24)

Take a few moments to intercede on behalf of your immediate family and other relatives. Offer prayers for their spiritual, emotional and physical concerns.

Affirmation

Your day, O Lord, will come like a thief. The heavens will pass away with a roar, and the elements will be destroyed by intense heat, and the earth and its works will be laid bare. Your day, O God, will bring about the destruction of the heavens by fire, and the elements will melt with intense heat. (2 Peter 3:10, 12)

There will be a new heaven and a new earth, for the first heaven and the first earth will pass away, and there will no longer be any sea. (Revelation 21:1)

Pause to reflect on these Biblical affirmations.

Thanksgiving

Lord, You said, "Let there be lights in the expanse of the heavens to separate the day from the night, and let them serve as signs to mark seasons and days and years, and let them be lights in the expanse of the heavens to give light on the earth"; and it was so. You made two great lights—the greater light to govern the day and the lesser light to govern the night. You also made the stars; You set them in the expanse of the heavens to give light on the earth, and to govern the day and the night, and to separate the light from the darkness. And You saw that it was good. (Genesis 1:14–19)

> You made the earth and created people upon it.
> Your own hands stretched out the heavens,
> And You ordered their starry hosts. (Isaiah 45:12)

Pause to offer your own expressions of thanksgiving.

Closing Prayer

> All Your works will praise you, O Lord,
> And Your saints will bless You.
> They will speak of the glory of Your kingdom
> And talk of Your power,
> So that all people may know of Your mighty acts
> And the glorious majesty of Your kingdom.
> Your kingdom is an everlasting kingdom,

And Your dominion endures through all generations.
   (Psalm 145:10–13)

Be exalted, O God, above the heavens,
And let Your glory be over all the earth. (Psalm 108:5)

DAY 31

Adoration

Your word, O Lord, is upright,
And all Your work is done in faithfulness.
You love righteousness and justice;
The earth is full of Your lovingkindness. (Psalm 33:4–5)

One thing You have spoken, O Lord,
Two things I have heard:
That You, O God, are strong
And that You, O Lord, are loving.
For You reward each person according to what he has
    done. (Psalm 62:11–12)

Pause to express your thoughts of praise and worship.

Confession

When I have sinned against You, and when I have turned
back to You and confessed my sin, hear from heaven and forgive my sin and restore me. Teach me the good way in which
I should walk. When I sin against You—for there is no one
who does not sin—may I return to You with all my heart
and with all my soul. (1 Kings 8:33–34, 36, 46, 48)

*Ask the Spirit to search your heart and reveal any areas of
unconfessed sin. Acknowledge these to the Lord and thank Him
for His forgiveness.*

Renewal

Like Noah, may I be a righteous person, blameless among the
people of my time, and one who walks with You. (Genesis 6:9)

Like Moses, may I do all that You command me. (Exodus
39:42; 40:16)

Pause to add your own prayers for personal renewal.

Petition

> O Lord, be not far off;
> O my Strength, come quickly to help me. (Psalm 22:19)

Pause here to petition God for spiritual insight so that you might have understanding of His Word. Ask for insight into your identity in Jesus Christ: that you might know who you are, what direction your life should take and what His purpose for your life is. Offer prayers regarding your activities for this day and any special concerns you may have.

Intercession

Lord, help us to bear one another's burdens and so fulfill the law of Christ. (Galatians 6:2)

Take a few moments to intercede on behalf of other believers, such as your personal friends, those in ministry and those who are oppressed and in need.

Affirmation

> You are my lamp, O Lord;
> You turn my darkness into light.
> With Your help I can advance against a troop;
> With You I can leap over a wall. (2 Samuel 22:29–30)

> You know the way that I take;
> When You have tested me, I shall come forth as gold.
> My feet have held fast to Your steps;
> I have kept to Your way without turning aside.
> (Job 23:10–11)

Pause to reflect on these Biblical affirmations.

Thanksgiving

In the beginning You created the heavens and the earth. When the earth was formless and empty, and darkness was over the surface of the deep, Your Spirit hovered over the face of the waters. And You said, "Let there be light," and there was light. Then You said, "Let there be an expanse in the midst of the waters, and let it separate the waters from the waters." So You made the expanse and separated the waters under the expanse from the waters above it, and it was so. Then You said, "Let the waters under the heavens be gathered into one place, and let dry ground appear"; and it was so. And You saw that it was good. (Genesis 1:1–10)

Pause to offer your own expressions of thanksgiving.

Closing Prayer

Let all who fear You, O Lord, come and listen,
And I will tell them what You have done for my soul.
I cried out to You with my mouth;
Your praise was on my tongue.
If I had regarded iniquity in my heart,
You would not have heard.
But You have surely heard;
You have attended to the voice of my prayer.
Praise be to You, O God.
You have neither turned away my prayer
Nor Your love from me! (Psalm 66:16–20)

THE SECOND MONTH

DAY 1

Adoration

O Lord, You cover Yourself in light as with a garment;
You stretch out the heavens like a tent curtain
And lay the beams of Your upper chambers in the waters.
You make the clouds Your chariot
And walk on the wings of the wind.
You make the winds Your messengers,
Flames of fire Your servants.
You set the earth on its foundations
So that it can never be moved.
You covered it with the deep as with a garment;
The waters stood above the mountains.
At Your rebuke the waters fled;
At the sound of Your thunder they hurried away.
They flowed over the mountains
And went down into the valleys,
To the place You assigned for them.
You set a boundary they cannot cross,
That they will not return to cover the earth.
O Lord, how manifold are Your works!
In wisdom You made them all;
The earth is full of Your possessions. (Psalm 104:2–9, 24)

Pause to express your thoughts of praise and worship.

Confession

You are wise in heart and mighty in strength, O God.
Who has resisted You without harm? (Job 9:4)

Ask the Spirit to search your heart and reveal any areas of unconfessed sin. Acknowledge these to the Lord and thank Him for His forgiveness.

Renewal

Examine me, O Lord, and try me;
Purify my mind and my heart;
For Your lovingkindness is ever before me,
And I walk in Your truth. (Psalm 26:2–3)

May I sow righteousness,
Reap the fruit of unfailing love,
And break up my fallow ground;
For it is time to seek You, O Lord,
Until You come and rain righteousness on me.
(Hosea 10:12)

Pause to add your own prayers for personal renewal.

Petition

O Lord, hear my prayer;
Listen to the voice of my supplications.
In the day of my trouble I will call upon You,
For You will answer me.
You are great and do wondrous deeds;
You alone are God. (Psalm 86:6–7, 10)

Pause here to petition God for growth in love and compassion toward others. Offer prayers for your loved ones, for those who do not know Jesus and for those in need. Offer prayers regarding your activities for this day and any special concerns you may have.

Intercession

May I sanctify You, O Christ, as Lord in my heart; may I always be ready to give an answer to everyone who asks me, to give the reason for the hope that is in me, but with gentleness and respect. (1 Peter 3:15)

Take a few moments to intercede on behalf of friends, relatives, neighbors and coworkers who do not yet know salvation in Jesus Christ.

Affirmation

Sin shall not be my master, because I am not under law, but under grace. I have been set free from sin and have become a slave of righteousness. (Romans 6:14, 18)

Jesus, You have taught us that those who have Your commandments and obey them are the ones who love You; and those who love You will be loved by Your Father, and You will love them and manifest Yourself to them. (John 14:21)

Pause to reflect on these Biblical affirmations.

Thanksgiving

Lord, You said, "Let Us make people in Our image, in Our likeness, and let them rule over the fish of the sea and the birds of the air and over the livestock and over all the earth and over all the creatures that creep on the earth." So You created people in Your own image; male and female You created them. Then You blessed them and said to them, "Be fruitful and multiply; fill the earth and subdue it; and rule over the fish of the sea and the birds of the air and over every living creature that moves on the earth." Then You said, "Behold, I have given you every seed-bearing plant on the face of the whole earth and every tree that has fruit with seed in it; they will be yours for food. And to all the beasts of the earth and all the birds of the air and all the creatures that move on the ground, in which there is life, I have given every green plant for food"; and it was so. You saw all that You had made, and it was very good. (Genesis 1:26–31)

Pause to offer your own expressions of thanksgiving.

Closing Prayer

May Your favor, O Lord our God, rest upon us,
And establish the work of our hands for us—
Yes, confirm the work of our hands. (Psalm 90:17)

DAY 2

Adoration

As the deer pants for the water brooks,
So my soul pants for You, O God.
My soul thirsts for You, the living God.
When shall I come and appear before You? (Psalm 42:1–2)

My soul yearns for You in the night;
My spirit within me diligently seeks You.
When Your judgments come upon the earth,
The inhabitants of the world learn righteousness.
   (Isaiah 26:9)

Pause to express your thoughts of praise and worship.

Confession

You are the righteous God,
   who searches hearts and secret thoughts. (Psalm 7:9)

Your lamp, O Lord, searches my spirit;
It searches the inward depths of my being.
   (Proverbs 20:27)

Ask the Spirit to search your heart and reveal any areas of unconfessed sin. Acknowledge these to the Lord and thank Him for His forgiveness.

Renewal

With regard to my former way of life, may I put off my old self, which is being corrupted by its deceitful desires, and be renewed in the spirit of my mind; and may I put on the new self, which was created to be like You, O God, in righteousness and true holiness. (Ephesians 4:22–24)

May I be diligent to add to my faith, virtue; and to virtue, knowledge; and to knowledge, self-control; and to self-control, perseverance; and to perseverance, godliness; and to godliness, brotherly kindness; and to brotherly kindness, love. For if these qualities are mine in increasing measure, they will keep me from being barren and unfruitful in the full knowledge of You, my Lord Jesus Christ. (2 Peter 1:5–8)

Pause to add your own prayers for personal renewal.

Petition

May I discipline myself to godliness. For physical exercise profits a little, but godliness is profitable for all things, since it holds promise for both the present life and the life to come. (1 Timothy 4:7–8)

Pause here to petition God to help you be a faithful steward of your time, talents, possessions and relationships. Offer prayers of petition regarding your activities for this day and any special concerns you may have.

Intercession

May I give to all what they are due: taxes to whom taxes are due, custom to whom custom, respect to whom respect, honor to whom honor. (Romans 13:7)

Take a few moments to intercede on behalf of your local, state or provincial, and national governments. Pray for spiritual revival in the nation and offer prayers regarding current events and concerns.

Affirmation

Those who pursue righteousness and love
Find life, righteousness and honor. (Proverbs 21:21)

Those who heed instruction prosper,
And blessed are those who trust in You, O Lord.
  (Proverbs 16:20)

Pause to reflect on these Biblical affirmations.

Thanksgiving

You are the Lord our God, who brought Your people out of
Egypt, out of the land of slavery. (Exodus 20:2)

Was it not You who dried up the sea,
The waters of the great deep;
Who made the depths of the sea a road
So that the redeemed might cross over? (Isaiah 51:10)

Pause to offer your own expressions of thanksgiving.

Closing Prayer

You are the Lord who created the heavens; You are God.
You fashioned and made the earth and established it;
You did not create it to be empty,
But formed it to be inhabited.
You are the Lord, and there is no other. (Isaiah 45:18)

You are in Your holy temple;
Let all the earth be silent before You. (Habakkuk 2:20)

DAY 3

Adoration

> Not to us, O Lord, not to us,
> But to Your name be glory,
> Because of Your lovingkindness and truth.
>   (Psalm 115:1)

> We give praise to You, Lord!
> For it is good to sing praises to You, our God,
> Because praise is pleasant and beautiful. (Psalm 147:1)

Pause to express your thoughts of praise and worship.

Confession

> You have set our iniquities before You, Lord,
> Our secret sins in the light of Your presence.
>   (Psalm 90:8)

Ask the Spirit to search your heart and reveal any areas of unconfessed sin. Acknowledge these to the Lord and thank Him for His forgiveness.

Renewal

May I fight the good fight of faith and lay hold of the eternal life to which I was called, Father, when I made the good confession in the presence of many witnesses. You are the One who gives life to all things; in Your sight, and in the sight of Your Son, Christ Jesus, who testified the good confession before Pontius Pilate, may I keep this command without blemish or reproach until the appearing of my Lord Jesus Christ, which You will bring about in Your own time. (1 Timothy 6:12–15)

O God, may I be diligent to present myself to You as one approved, a worker who does not need to be ashamed and who correctly handles the word of truth. (2 Timothy 2:15)

Pause to add your own prayers for personal renewal.

Petition

> May You, O Sovereign Lord, deal well with me for Your
>   name's sake;
> Because of the goodness of Your mercy, deliver me.
>   (Psalm 109:21)

Pause here to offer prayers of petition regarding your family and your ministry. Ask for help and guidance in sharing Jesus with others and helping others grow in Him. Ask for guidance in your vocation and your avocations. Offer prayers of petition regarding your activities for this day and any special concerns you may have.

Intercession

This is pure and undefiled religion before You, my God and Father: to visit orphans and widows in their affliction and to keep myself unspotted from the world. (James 1:27)

Take a few moments to intercede on behalf of local, national and world missions. Pray that the Great Commission would be fulfilled and for any special concerns you may have for missions.

Affirmation

No one can see Your kingdom, O God, without being born again; no one can enter into Your kingdom without being born of water and Your Spirit. That which is born of the flesh is flesh, and that which is born of the Spirit is spirit. The wind blows wherever it pleases, and we hear its sound, but we cannot tell where it comes from, or where it is going. So it is with everyone born of the Spirit. (John 3:3, 5–6, 8)

O Lord, through Your Spirit, by faith, I eagerly await the righteousness for which I hope. (Galatians 5:5)

Pause to reflect on these Biblical affirmations.

Thanksgiving

> I will give thanks to You, O Lord, and call upon Your
>   name,
> And make known to others what You have done.
> I will sing to You, sing praises to You,
> And tell of all Your wonderful acts. (1 Chronicles 16:8–9)
>
> O Lord, I know that You have set apart the godly for
>   Yourself;
> You hear when I call to You. (Psalm 4:3)

Pause to offer your own expressions of thanksgiving.

Closing Prayer

God highly exalted You, Christ Jesus, and gave You the name that is above every name, that at Your name every knee should bow, in heaven and on earth and under the earth, and every tongue should confess that You, Jesus Christ, are Lord, to the glory of God the Father. (Philippians 2:9–11)

I give honor and praise to You, O Christ, the head of the body, the church; for You are the beginning and the first-born from among the dead, so that in everything You might have the supremacy. (Colossians 1:18)

DAY 4

Adoration

Who has understood what is in Your mind, O Lord,
Or instructed You as Your counselor?
Whom did You consult to enlighten You,
And who taught You the path of justice?
Who taught You knowledge
Or showed You the way of understanding?
Surely the nations are like a drop in a bucket
And are regarded as dust on the scales;
You weigh the islands as though they were fine dust.
Before You all the nations are as nothing;
You regard them as less than nothing and worthless.
To whom, then, will I compare You?
Or what likeness will I compare with You?
    (Isaiah 40:13–15, 17–18)

Pause to express your thoughts of praise and worship.

Confession

Who among us fears You, O Lord,
And obeys the word of Your Servant?
Let those who walk in darkness and have no light
Trust in Your name, O Lord, and rely upon You.
    (Isaiah 50:10)

*Ask the Spirit to search your heart and reveal any areas of
unconfessed sin. Acknowledge these to the Lord and thank Him
for His forgiveness.*

Renewal

By Your grace, I want to observe Your judgments and keep
Your statutes, to walk in them; You are the Lord my God.

May I keep Your statutes and Your judgments, for the one who obeys them will live by them. You are the Lord. (Leviticus 18:4–5)

May I fear You, O Lord, and serve and obey You and not rebel against Your commands. (1 Samuel 12:14)

Pause to add your own prayers for personal renewal.

Petition

May I not imitate what is evil but what is good. The one who does good is of God; the one who does evil has not seen You. (3 John 11)

Pause here to petition God for growth in your character and personal discipline, and for physical health and strength. Ask that He empower you for spiritual warfare against the temptations of the world, the flesh and the devil. Offer prayers regarding your activities for this day and any special concerns you may have.

Intercession

Lord, there is no one besides You to help the powerless against the mighty. Help us, O Lord our God, for we rest in You. O Lord, You are our God; do not let people prevail against You. (2 Chronicles 14:11)

Take a few moments to intercede on behalf of the poor and hungry, the oppressed and persecuted, and those in control of world and national resources. Offer prayers for peace among nations and regarding current events and concerns.

Affirmation

> You will keep in perfect peace those who commit
> themselves to be faithful to You,
> Because they trust in You. (Isaiah 26:3)

I will seek You, Lord, while You may be found
And call upon You while You are near. (Isaiah 55:6)

Pause to reflect on these Biblical affirmations.

Thanksgiving

I will give thanks to You, O Lord, because of Your
   righteousness
And will sing praise to Your name, Lord Most High.
   (Psalm 7:17)

You are my light and my salvation, O Lord;
Whom shall I fear?
You are the strength of my life;
Of whom shall I be afraid? (Psalm 27:1)

Pause to offer your own expressions of thanksgiving.

Closing Prayer

I will sing to You as long as I live;
I will sing praise to You, my God, while I have my
   being.
May my meditation be pleasing to You;
I will be glad in You, O Lord. (Psalm 104:33–34)

You give strength to the weary, O God,
And increase the power of the weak.
Even youths grow tired and weary,
And young men stumble and fall;
But those who wait for You
Will renew their strength;
They will mount up with wings like eagles;
They will run and not grow weary;
They will walk and not be faint. (Isaiah 40:29–31)

DAY 5

Adoration

> You are the true God;
> You are the living God and the everlasting King.
> At Your wrath, the earth trembles,
> And the nations cannot endure Your indignation.
>   (Jeremiah 10:10)

> How great are Your signs, O God,
> And how mighty are Your wonders!
> Your kingdom is an eternal kingdom;
> Your dominion endures from generation to generation.
>   (Daniel 4:3)

Pause to express your thoughts of praise and worship.

Confession

May I produce fruit in keeping with repentance. (Matthew 3:8)

Ask the Spirit to search your heart and reveal any areas of unconfessed sin. Acknowledge these to the Lord and thank Him for His forgiveness.

Renewal

> Teach me to number my days,
> That I may gain a heart of wisdom. (Psalm 90:12)

> May I let my eyes look straight ahead
> And fix my gaze straight before me.
> May I ponder the path of my feet
> So that all my ways will be established.
> May I not turn to the right or to the left
> But keep my foot from evil. (Proverbs 4:25–27)

Pause to add your own prayers for personal renewal.

Petition

> Hear my prayer, O Lord,
> Give ear to my supplications!
> Answer me in Your faithfulness and righteousness.
>   (Psalm 143:1)

Pause here to petition God for growth in your desire to know and please Jesus Christ. Pray for a greater love and commitment to Him, for the grace to practice His presence and for the grace to glorify Him in your life. Offer prayers regarding your activities for this day and any special concerns you may have.

Intercession

O Lord, we acknowledge that there are different kinds of gifts, but they are given by the same Spirit. And there are different kinds of service, but the same Lord. And there are different kinds of working, but You are the same God who works all of them in all people. But to each one the manifestation of the Spirit is given for the common good. (1 Corinthians 12:4–7)

Take a few moments to intercede on behalf of your local church, other churches, evangelism and discipleship ministries, educational ministries and any other special concerns you may have.

Affirmation

No one can lay a foundation other than the one already laid; You are the foundation, O Jesus Christ. (1 Corinthians 3:11)

It is by faith that I stand firm. (2 Corinthians 1:24)

Knowing that a person is not justified by the works of the law, but through faith in You, Christ Jesus, I have believed in You, that I may be justified through faith in You and not by the works of the law; for by the works of the law no flesh will be justified. (Galatians 2:16)

Pause to reflect on these Biblical affirmations.

Thanksgiving

O Lord my God, many are the wonders You have done,
And Your thoughts toward us no one can recount to You;
Were I to speak and tell of them,
They would be too many to declare. (Psalm 40:5)

I will praise You forever for what You have done;
I will hope in Your name, for it is good.
I will praise You in the presence of Your saints.
   (Psalm 52:9)

Pause to offer your own expressions of thanksgiving.

Closing Prayer

I know that all things work together for good to those who love You, O God, to those who have been called according to Your purpose. (Romans 8:28)

O God, if You are for me, who can be against me? You who did not spare Your own Son, but delivered Him up for us all, how will You not, along with Him, freely give us all things? (Romans 8:31–32)

Adoration

You, O Holy One, have asked,
"To whom will you compare Me?
Or who is My equal?"
We lift our eyes to the heavens
And see Who has created them.
You bring out the starry host by number
And call them each by name.
Because of Your great might and the strength of Your
  power,
Not one of them is missing.
Do we not know? Have we not heard?
You are the everlasting God, the Lord, the Creator of
  the ends of the earth.
You do not grow tired or weary.
No one can fathom Your understanding.
  (Isaiah 40:25–26, 28)

You, O Lord, reign forever;
Your throne endures from generation to generation.
  (Lamentations 5:19)

Pause to express your thoughts of praise and worship.

Confession

Why should we complain
When punished for our sins?
Let us search out and examine our ways,
And let us return to You, O Lord.
  (Lamentations 3:39–40)

Ask the Spirit to search your heart and reveal any areas of unconfessed sin. Acknowledge these to the Lord and thank Him for His forgiveness.

Renewal

> May I apply my heart to instruction
> And my ears to words of knowledge. (Proverbs 23:12)

May I watch and pray so that I will not fall into temptation; my spirit is willing, but my flesh is weak. (Matthew 26:41)

Pause to add your own prayers for personal renewal.

Petition

May I keep Your statutes and Your commandments and be careful to do as You, O Lord my God, have commanded me; may I not turn aside to the right or to the left. (Deuteronomy 4:40; 5:32)

Pause here to petition God for wisdom. Ask Him to develop your eternal perspective, to renew your mind with truth and to help you develop greater skill in each area of your life. Offer prayers regarding your activities for this day and any special concerns you may have.

Intercession

If I speak in the languages of humans and of angels, but have not love, I am only a resounding gong or a clanging cymbal. And if I have the gift of prophecy and understand all mysteries and all knowledge, and if I have all faith so as to remove mountains, but have not love, I am nothing. And if I give all my possessions to the poor, and if I deliver my body to be burned, but have not love, it profits me nothing. (1 Corinthians 13:1–3)

Take a few moments to intercede on behalf of your immediate family and other relatives. Offer prayers for their spiritual, emotional and physical concerns.

Affirmation

I am no longer a stranger and alien, but a fellow citizen with Your people and a member of Your household, O God, that was built on the foundation of the apostles and prophets, with Christ Jesus Himself as the chief cornerstone. (Ephesians 2:19–20)

I have been called, having been loved by You, God my Father, and kept by Jesus Christ. (Jude 1)

Pause to reflect on these Biblical affirmations.

Thanksgiving

You answer us with awesome deeds of righteousness,
O God of our salvation,
You who are the hope of all the ends of the earth
And of the farthest seas;
You formed the mountains by Your strength,
Having armed Yourself with power;
And You stilled the roaring of the seas,
The roaring of their waves,
And the tumult of the peoples. (Psalm 65:5–7)

Pause to offer your own expressions of thanksgiving.

Closing Prayer

Better is one day in Your courts than a thousand
    elsewhere;
I would rather be a doorkeeper in Your house
Than dwell in the tents of the wicked.

For You, Lord God, are a sun and shield;
You will give grace and glory;
No good thing do You withhold
From those who walk in integrity.
O Lord of hosts,
Blessed is the one who trusts in You! (Psalm 84:10–12)

DAY 7

Adoration

We confess that in the beginning was the Word, and the Word was with You, O God, and the Word was You. The Word was in the beginning with You. (John 1:1–2)

You are but one God, the Father from whom all things came and for whom I live; and there is but one Lord Jesus Christ, through whom all things came and through whom I live. (1 Corinthians 8:6)

Pause to express your thoughts of praise and worship.

Confession

I know that You are a gracious and compassionate God, slow to anger and abounding in lovingkindness; You are a God who relents from sending calamity. (Jonah 4:2)

Ask the Spirit to search your heart and reveal any areas of unconfessed sin. Acknowledge these to the Lord and thank Him for His forgiveness.

Renewal

May I not be like the rocky places on which seed was thrown—like those who hear the word and at once receive it with joy, but since they have no root, last only a short time; when affliction or persecution comes because of the word, they quickly fall away. And may I not be like soil among the thorns on which seed was sown—like those who hear the word, but the worries of this world, the deceitfulness of riches and pleasures, and the desires for other things come in and choke the word, making it immature and unfruitful. Instead, may I be like the good soil on which seed was sown, like those who with noble and good hearts hear the word, understand and accept it, and with perseverance bear fruit, yielding thirty, sixty or a hundred times what was sown. (Matthew 13:20–23; Mark 4:16–20; Luke 8:13–15)

Pause to add your own prayers for personal renewal.

Petition

If we die, will we live again?
All the days of my hard service
I will wait for my renewal to come. (Job 14:14)

Pause here to petition God for spiritual insight so that you might have understanding of His Word. Ask for insight into your identity in Jesus Christ: that you might know who you are, what direction your life should take and what His purpose for your life is. Offer prayers regarding your activities for this day and any special concerns you may have.

Intercession

All of us have become like those who are unclean,
And all our righteous acts are like filthy rags;
We all shrivel up like leaves,
And our iniquities, like the wind, sweep us away.
But now, O Lord, You are our Father.
We are the clay, You are the potter;
We are all the work of Your hand. (Isaiah 64:6, 8)

Take a few moments to intercede on behalf of other believers, such as your personal friends, those in ministry and those who are oppressed and in need.

Affirmation

Like Abram, when I believe in Your promises, You will credit it to me as righteousness. (Genesis 15:5–6)

Whatever things were written in the past were written for our learning, so that through endurance and the encouragement of the Scriptures we might have hope. (Romans 15:4)

Like Abraham, I am waiting for a city that You have planned and built, O God. (Hebrews 11:10)

Pause to reflect on these Biblical affirmations.

Thanksgiving

I will praise You, O Lord my God, with all my heart,
And I will glorify Your name forever.
For great is Your love toward me,
And You have delivered my soul from the depths of the
    grave. (Psalm 86:12–13)

All who are righteous rejoice in You, O Lord,
And give thanks at the remembrance of Your holy
    name. (Psalm 97:12)

Pause to offer your own expressions of thanksgiving.

Closing Prayer

I love You, O Lord, my strength.
You are my rock and my fortress and my deliverer;
You are my rock, in whom I take refuge.
You are my shield and the horn of my salvation, my
    stronghold.
I call upon You, for You are worthy of praise,
And I am saved from my enemies. (Psalm 18:1–3)

Many are the sorrows of the wicked,
But the one who trusts in You, O Lord, will be
    surrounded by Your lovingkindness. (Psalm 32:10)

DAY 8

Adoration

> You, O God, bind the cluster of the Pleiades
> And loose the cords of Orion.
> You, O God, bring forth the constellations in their
>   seasons
> And guide the Bear with its cubs.
> You know the ordinances of the heavens
> And set their dominion over the earth. (Job 38:31–33)
>
> I know that You can do all things
> And that no purpose of Yours can be thwarted. (Job 42:2)

Pause to express your thoughts of praise and worship.

Confession

> I know, O Lord, that my life is not my own;
> It is not for me to direct my steps.
> O Lord, correct me, but with justice—
> Not in Your anger, lest You reduce me to nothing.
>   (Jeremiah 10:23–24)

Ask the Spirit to search your heart and reveal any areas of unconfessed sin. Acknowledge these to the Lord and thank Him for His forgiveness.

Renewal

> May I receive the words of wisdom
> And treasure her commands within me,
> Turning my ear to wisdom
> And applying my heart to understanding.
> If I cry for discernment
> And lift up my voice for understanding,

If I seek her as silver
And search for her as for hidden treasures,
Then I will understand what it is to fear You
And what it is to know You.
Then I will understand righteousness and justice and
     honesty—
Every good path.
For wisdom will enter my heart,
And knowledge will be pleasant to my soul.
Discretion will protect me,
and understanding will guard me. (Proverbs 2:1–5, 9–11)

Pause to add your own prayers for personal renewal.

Petition

Hear, O Lord, and be merciful to me;
O Lord, be my helper.
You turned my mourning into dancing;
You removed my sackcloth and clothed me with
     gladness,
That my heart may sing praise to You and not be silent.
O Lord my God, I will give thanks to You forever.
     (Psalm 30:10–12)

*Pause here to petition God for growth in love and compassion
toward others. Offer prayers for your loved ones, for those who
do not know Jesus and for those in need. Offer prayers regarding your activities for this day and any special concerns you may
have.*

Intercession

The harvest is plentiful, but the workers are few. Therefore,
I will pray that You, the Lord of the harvest, will send out
workers into Your harvest. (Matthew 9:37–38; Luke 10:2)

Take a few moments to intercede on behalf of friends, relatives, neighbors and coworkers who do not yet know salvation in Jesus Christ.

Affirmation

You are my hiding place and my shield;
I have put my hope in Your word. (Psalm 119:114)

Every word You speak is flawless, O God;
You are a shield to those who take refuge in You.
    (Proverbs 30:5)

Everything You have created eagerly waits in expectation of the time when Your children will appear in their full and final glory. (Romans 8:19)

Pause to reflect on these Biblical affirmations.

Thanksgiving

All the kings of the earth will give thanks to You, O Lord,
When they hear the words of Your mouth.
Yes, they sing of Your ways, O Lord,
For Your glory is great.
Though You reign on high,
Yet You look upon the lowly,
But the proud You know from afar. (Psalm 138:4–6)

Pause to offer your own expressions of thanksgiving.

Closing Prayer

My days are like a lengthened shadow,
And I wither away like grass.
But You, O Lord, will endure forever,
And the remembrance of Your name to all generations.

In the beginning You laid the foundations of the earth,
And the heavens are the work of Your hands.
They will perish, but You will endure;
They will all wear out like a garment.
Like clothing You will change them, and they will be
    discarded.
But You are the same,
And Your years will have no end.
    (Psalm 102:11–12, 25–27)

DAY 9

Adoration

> The earth is Yours, O Lord, and everything in it,
> The world and all who dwell in it.
> For You founded it upon the seas
> And established it upon the waters. (Psalm 24:1–2)

> You sit enthroned above the circle of the earth, O God,
> And its inhabitants are like grasshoppers.
> You stretch out the heavens like a curtain
> And spread them out like a tent to dwell in.
> You reduce rulers to nothing
> And make the judges of this world meaningless.
>   (Isaiah 40:22–23)

Pause to express your thoughts of praise and worship.

Confession

> The refining pot is for silver and the furnace for gold,
> But You, O Lord, test the heart. (Proverbs 17:3)

Ask the Spirit to search your heart and reveal any areas of unconfessed sin. Acknowledge these to the Lord and thank Him for His forgiveness.

Renewal

May I know You and serve You with my whole heart and with a willing mind; for You search all hearts and understand every motive behind the thoughts. (1 Chronicles 28:9)

May I imitate You, O God, as a beloved child, and walk in love, just as Christ loved me and gave Himself up for me as a fragrant offering and sacrifice to You. (Ephesians 5:1–2)

Pause to add your own prayers for personal renewal.

Petition

May I not love the world or the things in the world. If I love the world, Your love, O Father, is not in me. For all that is in the world—the lust of the flesh, the lust of the eyes, and the pride of life—is not of You, Father, but of the world. And the world and its lusts are passing away, but the one who does Your will abides forever. (1 John 2:15–17)

Pause here to petition God to help you be a faithful steward of your time, talents, possessions and relationships. Offer prayers of petition regarding your activities for this day and any special concerns you may have.

Intercession

You, O Lord, have said, "If My people, who are called by My name, will humble themselves and pray and seek My face and turn from their wicked ways, then I will hear from heaven and will forgive their sin and heal their land." (2 Chronicles 7:14)

Take a few moments to intercede on behalf of your local, state or provincial, and national governments. Pray for spiritual revival in the nation and offer prayers regarding current events and concerns.

Affirmation

I am not ashamed of the gospel, O God, for it is Your power for salvation to everyone who believes, to the Jew first, and also to the Gentile. For in it, a righteousness that is from You is revealed from faith to faith, just as it is written: "The righteous will live by faith." (Romans 1:16–17)

Clearly no one is justified before You, O God, by the law, for, "The righteous will live by faith." (Galatians 3:11)

Lord Jesus Christ, before faith in You came, we were guarded by the law, confined until the faith was later revealed. So the law has become our tutor to lead us to You, that we might be justified by faith. Now that faith has come, we are no longer under a tutor. (Galatians 3:23–25)

Pause to reflect on these Biblical affirmations.

Thanksgiving

You uphold all who fall, O Lord,
And lift up all who are bowed down.
The eyes of all look to You,
And You give them their food at the proper time.
You open Your hand
And satisfy the desire of every living thing.
    (Psalm 145:14–16)

Pause to offer your own expressions of thanksgiving.

Closing Prayer

You, Lord Jesus, are the first and the last and the Living One; You were dead, and behold, You are alive forevermore and hold the keys of death and of Hades. (Revelation 1:17–18)

Worthy are You, O Lamb of God, who were slain,
To receive power and riches and wisdom
And strength and honor and glory and blessing!
    (Revelation 5:12)

DAY 10

Adoration

> You are He; You are the first,
> And You are also the last. (Isaiah 48:12)

You, O God and Father of the Lord Jesus, are blessed forever. (2 Corinthians 11:31)

O God, the Son is the radiance of Your glory and the exact representation of Your being, upholding all things by His powerful word. After He cleansed our sins, He sat down at Your right hand, having become as much superior to angels as the name He has inherited is more excellent than theirs. (Hebrews 1:3–4)

Pause to express your thoughts of praise and worship.

Confession

> All my ways are before Your eyes, O Lord,
> And You examine all my paths. (Proverbs 5:21)

Ask the Spirit to search your heart and reveal any areas of unconfessed sin. Acknowledge these to the Lord and thank Him for His forgiveness.

Renewal

Since I live in You, Holy Spirit, may I also walk in You. (Galatians 5:25)

Father, may You fill me with the knowledge of Your will through all spiritual wisdom and understanding, so that I may live a life worthy of You and please You in every way, bearing fruit in every good work and growing in Your grace, strengthened with all power according to Your glorious might, so that I may have great endurance and patience with joy. (Colossians 1:9–11)

Pause to add your own prayers for personal renewal.

Petition

I cry out to You, O Lord,
And say, "You are my refuge,
My portion in the land of the living." (Psalm 142:5)

Pause here to offer prayers of petition regarding your family and your ministry. Ask for His help and guidance in sharing Jesus with others and helping others grow in Him. Ask for guidance in your vocation and your avocations. Offer prayers of petition regarding your activities for this day and any special concerns you may have.

Intercession

As You, Father, sent Your Son into the world, Your Son also has sent us into the world. And He has prayed for those who will believe in Him through our message. (John 17:18, 20)

Take a few moments to intercede on behalf of local, national and world missions. Pray that the Great Commission would be fulfilled and for any special concerns you may have for missions.

Affirmation

Like Jesus, dear Father, my food is to do Your will and to accomplish Your work. (John 4:34)

This is love: that I walk in obedience to Your commandments, O God. And this is the commandment that I have heard from the beginning: I should walk in love. (2 John 6)

Pause to reflect on these Biblical affirmations.

Thanksgiving

You, Lord God, will swallow up death forever,
And You will wipe away the tears from all faces;
You will remove the reproach of Your people from all
    the earth.
For You have spoken.
And it will be said in that day,
"Behold, this is our God;
We have waited for Him, and He will save us.
This is the Lord;
We have trusted in Him.
Let us rejoice and be glad in His salvation."
    (Isaiah 25:8–9)

Father, we look for the time when the Holy City, the new
Jerusalem, will come down out of heaven, prepared as a
bride adorned for her husband. A loud voice from the throne
will say, "Behold, God makes His home with people, and
He will dwell with them, and they will be His people, and
God Himself will be with them and be their God, and He
will wipe every tear from their eyes. There will be no more
death or mourning or crying or pain, for the first things have
passed away." You, the One who is seated on the throne, will
say, "Behold, I make all things new." (Revelation 21:2–5)

Pause to offer your own expressions of thanksgiving.

Closing Prayer

You have sworn by Yourself;
The word has gone out of Your mouth in righteousness
And will not return.
Every knee will bow before You,
And every tongue will acknowledge You. (Isaiah 45:23)

Lamb of God, You are worthy to take the scroll
And to open its seals,

Because You were slain;
And with Your blood You purchased us for God
From every tribe and language and people and nation.
You have made us to be a kingdom and priests to serve
    our God,
And we will reign on the earth. (Revelation 5:9–10)

DAY 11

Adoration

Your testimonies, which You have commanded,
Are righteous and trustworthy.
Your righteousness is everlasting,
And Your law is truth. (Psalm 119:138, 142)

My heart is steadfast, O God;
I will sing praises with all my soul.
Awake, harp and lyre!
I will awaken the dawn.
I will praise You, O Lord, among the peoples;
I will sing of You among the nations.
Your merciful love is higher than the heavens,
And Your truth reaches to the skies. (Psalm 108:1–4)

Pause to express your thoughts of praise and worship.

Confession

Blessed is the one You discipline, O Lord,
The one You teach from Your word. (Psalm 94:12)

Ask the Spirit to search your heart and reveal any areas of unconfessed sin. Acknowledge these to the Lord and thank Him for His forgiveness.

Renewal

You are God Almighty; may I walk before You and be blameless. (Genesis 17:1)

May I love my enemies, do good to them and lend to them, expecting nothing in return. Then my reward will be great and I will be Your child, O Most High; for You are kind to the ungrateful and evil. May I be merciful just as You are merciful. (Luke 6:35–36)

Pause to add your own prayers for personal renewal.

Petition

May I not be dishonest in judgment, in measurement of weight or quantity. May I be honest and just in my business affairs. (Leviticus 19:35–36)

Pause here to petition God for growth in your character and personal discipline, and for physical health and strength. Ask that He empower you for spiritual warfare against the temptations of the world, the flesh and the devil. Offer prayers regarding your activities for this day and any special concerns you may have.

Intercession

You, O Lord, have declared that we must:
"Defend the weak and the fatherless;
Do justice to the afflicted and destitute.
Rescue the poor and needy and
Deliver them from the hand of the wicked."
(Psalm 82:3–4)

Take a few moments to intercede on behalf of the poor and hungry, the oppressed and persecuted, and those in control of world and national resources. Offer prayers for peace among nations and regarding current events and concerns.

Affirmation

I am not trying to win the approval of other people; I want to win Your approval, Lord. If I were still trying to please people, I would not be a servant of Christ. (Galatians 1:10)

If I am afraid of people, fear will trap me.
But if I trust in You, O Lord, You will keep me safe.
   (Proverbs 29:25)

My help comes from You, O Lord,
Who made heaven and earth. (Psalm 124:8)

Pause to reflect on these Biblical affirmations.

Thanksgiving

Since Your children have partaken of flesh and blood, You also, O Christ, shared in their humanity so that by Your death You might destroy him who holds the power of death—the devil—and free those who all their lives were held in slavery by their fear of death. (Hebrews 2:14–15)

We thank You, Jesus Christ, that You were made like Your brothers and sisters in every way, in order that You might become a merciful and faithful high priest in things pertaining to God, to make propitiation for our sins. Because You Yourself suffered when You were tempted, You are able to help those of us who are being tempted. (Hebrews 2:17–18)

Pause to offer your own expressions of thanksgiving.

Closing Prayer

   Blessed are those who do not walk in the counsel of the
      wicked
   Or stand in the way of sinners
   Or sit in the seat of scorners.
   But their delight is in Your law, O Lord,
   And on Your law they meditate day and night.
   And they shall be like trees planted by streams of water,
   Which yield fruit in due season
   And whose leaves do not wither;
   Whatever they do will prosper. (Psalm 1:1–3)

DAY 12

Adoration

> Great are You, Lord, and most worthy of praise
> In Your city, Your holy mountain.
> We have meditated on Your unfailing love, O God,
> In the midst of Your temple.
> As is Your name, O God,
> So is Your praise to the ends of the earth;
> Your right hand is filled with righteousness.
>   (Psalm 48:1, 9–10)
>
> We come, we worship and we bow down,
> We kneel before You, the Lord our Maker. (Psalm 95:6)

Pause to express your thoughts of praise and worship.

Confession

> How can I discern my errors?
> Cleanse me from hidden faults.
> Keep Your servant also from presumptuous sins;
> Let them not rule over me.
> Then will I be blameless,
> And innocent of great transgression. (Psalm 19:12–13)

Ask the Spirit to search your heart and reveal any areas of unconfessed sin. Acknowledge these to the Lord and thank Him for His forgiveness.

Renewal

Lord, you have taught us that love is patient, love is kind, it does not envy; love does not boast, it is not arrogant, it does not behave rudely; it does not seek its own, it is not provoked, it keeps no record of wrongs; it does not rejoice in unrighteousness but rejoices with the truth; it bears all things, believes all things, hopes all things, endures all things. Love never fails. (1 Corinthians 13:4–8)

May my love abound more and more in full knowledge and depth of insight, so that I may be able to approve the things that are excellent, in order to be sincere and blameless until the day of Christ—having been filled with the fruit of righteousness that comes through Jesus Christ, to Your glory and praise, O God. (Philippians 1:9–11)

Pause to add your own prayers for personal renewal.

Petition

Since I died with You, Jesus, to the basic principles of this world, may I not submit to the world's regulations as though I still belonged to it. (Colossians 2:20)

Pause here to petition God for growth in your desire to know and please Jesus Christ. Pray for a greater love and commitment to Him, for the grace to practice His presence and for the grace to glorify Him in your life. Offer prayers regarding your activities for this day and any special concerns you may have.

Intercession

Lord, we know that there should be no division in the body, but its members should have concern for each other. If one member suffers, all the members suffer with it; if one member is honored, all the members rejoice with it. Now we are Your body, Jesus, and each one of us is a member of it. (1 Corinthians 12:25–27)

Take a few moments to intercede on behalf of your local church, other churches, evangelism and discipleship ministries, educational ministries and any other special concerns you may have.

Affirmation

I am not competent in myself to claim anything for myself, but my competence comes from You, O God. You have made me competent as a minister of a new covenant, not of the letter, but of Your Spirit; for the letter kills, but Your Spirit gives life. (2 Corinthians 3:5–6)

It is because of You, Father, that I am in Christ Jesus, who has become for me wisdom from You—that is, my righteousness, sanctification and redemption. (1 Corinthians 1:30)

Pause to reflect on these Biblical affirmations.

Thanksgiving

It is in You, Lord Jesus, that I have peace. In this world I will have tribulation, but I will be of good cheer, because You have overcome the world. (John 16:33)

I have been set apart for Your gospel, O God—I am among those who are called to belong to Jesus Christ. (Romans 1:1, 6)

Pause to offer your own expressions of thanksgiving.

Closing Prayer

O Lord, You are my shepherd;
I shall not be in want.
You make me lie down in green pastures;
You lead me beside quiet waters;
You restore my soul.
You guide me in the paths of righteousness
For Your name's sake.
Even though I walk through the valley of the shadow of
    death,
I will fear no evil, for You are with me;
Your rod and Your staff, they comfort me.

You prepare a table before me in the presence of my
    enemies.
You anoint my head with oil;
My cup overflows.
Surely goodness and mercy will follow me all the days
    of my life,
And I will dwell in Your house forever. (Psalm 23:1–6)

DAY 13

Adoration

Lord God of hosts—
You who touch the earth and it melts,
And all who live in it mourn;
You who build Your staircase in the heavens
And set its foundation on the earth;
You who call for the waters of the sea
And pour them out over the face of the earth—
The Lord is Your name. (Amos 9:5–6)

All flesh is silent before You, O Lord, for You are aroused from Your holy dwelling place. (Zechariah 2:13)

Pause to express your thoughts of praise and worship.

Confession

Have mercy on me, O God,
According to Your loyal love;
According to the greatness of Your compassion
Blot out my transgressions.
Wash me completely from my iniquity
And cleanse me from my sin.
For I know my transgressions,
And my sin is ever before me.
Against You, You only, have I sinned
And done what is evil in Your sight,
So that You are justified when You speak
And blameless when You judge. (Psalm 51:1–4)

Ask the Spirit to search your heart and reveal any areas of unconfessed sin. Acknowledge these to the Lord and thank Him for His forgiveness.

Renewal

May I not work for the food that perishes, but for the food that endures to eternal life, which the Son of Man gives me, for You, Father, have set Your seal on Him. (John 6:27)

Whatever was gain to me I now consider loss for Your sake, O Christ. What is more, I consider all things loss compared to the surpassing greatness of knowing You as my Lord; for Your sake I suffer the loss of all things and consider them rubbish, that I may gain You and be found in You, not having a righteousness of my own that comes from the law, but that which is through faith in You—the righteousness that comes from God on the basis of faith. (Philippians 3:7–9)

Pause to add your own prayers for personal renewal.

Petition

Rise up, O Lord!
May Your enemies be scattered,
And may those who hate You flee before You.
(Numbers 10:35)

Pause here to petition God for wisdom. Ask Him to develop your eternal perspective, to renew your mind with truth and to help you develop greater skill in each area of your life. Offer prayers regarding your activities for this day and any special concerns you may have.

Intercession

May we keep Your feast, O Christ our Passover, not with old leaven, or with the leaven of malice and wickedness, but with the unleavened bread of sincerity and truth. (1 Corinthians 5:7–8)

Take a few moments to intercede on behalf of your immediate family and other relatives. Offer prayers for their spiritual, emotional and physical concerns.

Affirmation

Those who are without your Spirit do not accept the things of Your Spirit, which are foolishness to them, and they cannot understand them, for such things are spiritually discerned. "For who has known Your mind, O Lord, that he may instruct You?" But we have the mind of Christ. (1 Corinthians 2:14, 16)

Now I see dimly, as in a mirror, but then I shall see face to face. Now I know in part, but then I shall know fully, even as I am fully known. (1 Corinthians 13:12)

Pause to reflect on these Biblical affirmations.

Thanksgiving

You will keep me strong to the end, so that I will be blameless on the day of our Lord Jesus Christ. You are faithful; You have called me into fellowship with Your Son, Jesus Christ our Lord. (1 Corinthians 1:8–9)

No eye has seen, no ear has heard, no mind has conceived, O God, what You have prepared for those who love You. (1 Corinthians 2:9)

Pause to offer your own expressions of thanksgiving.

Closing Prayer

Lord, make me to know my end
And what is the measure of my days;
Let me know how fleeting is my life. (Psalm 39:4)

You know how I am formed;
You remember that I am dust.
People's days are like grass;
People flourish like flowers of the field.
The wind passes over them and they are gone,

And their place remembers them no more.
But Your lovingkindness is from everlasting to
    everlasting
To those who fear You,
And Your righteousness with their children's children,
To those who keep Your covenant
And remember to obey Your precepts. (Psalm 103:14–18)

DAY 14

Adoration

O Lord, You reign; You are clothed with majesty;
You are robed in majesty and are armed with strength.
Indeed, the world is firmly established; it cannot be
    moved.
Your throne is established from of old;
You are from everlasting.
Your testimonies stand firm;
Holiness adorns Your house,
O Lord, forever. (Psalm 93:1–2, 5)

My soul blesses You, O Lord my God,
You are very great;
You are clothed with splendor and majesty. (Psalm 104:1)

Pause to express your thoughts of praise and worship.

Confession

If I claim to be without sin, I deceive myself and the truth
is not in me. If I confess my sins, You are faithful and just
and will forgive me my sins and purify me from all unrighteousness. If I claim I have not sinned, I make You out to be
a liar and Your word is not in me. (1 John 1:8–10)

*Ask the Spirit to search your heart and reveal any areas of
unconfessed sin. Acknowledge these to the Lord and thank Him
for His forgiveness.*

Renewal

Teach me to do Your will,
For You are my God;
May Your good Spirit lead me on level ground.
    (Psalm 143:10)

May I listen to counsel and accept instruction,
That I may be wise in my latter days. (Proverbs 19:20)

Pause to add your own prayers for personal renewal.

Petition

May I be strong and courageous; may I not be afraid or discouraged because of my adversaries; there is a greater power with me than with them, for You, Lord my God, are with me to help me. (2 Chronicles 32:7–8)

Pause here to petition God for spiritual insight so that you might have understanding of His Word. Ask for insight into your identity in Jesus Christ: that you might know who you are, what direction your life should take and what His purpose for your life is. Offer prayers regarding your activities for this day and any special concerns you may have.

Intercession

I was called to freedom, but may I not use my freedom to indulge the flesh; but through love let me serve others. For the whole law is summed up in these words: "You shall love your neighbor as yourself." (Galatians 5:13–14)

Take a few moments to intercede on behalf of other believers, such as your personal friends, those in ministry and those who are oppressed and in need.

Affirmation

O God, who will bring a charge against those whom You have chosen? You are the One who justifies. Who is he who condemns? It is Christ Jesus who died, who was furthermore raised to life, who is at Your right hand and is also interceding for me. (Romans 8:33–34)

An hour is coming, Father, and now is, when the dead will hear the voice of Your Son, and those who hear will live. For as You have life in Yourself, so You have granted the Son to have life in Himself, and You have given Him authority to execute judgment, because He is the Son of Man. (John 5:25–27)

Pause to reflect on these Biblical affirmations.

Thanksgiving

> You are close to the brokenhearted, Lord,
> And save those who are crushed in spirit.
> Many are the afflictions of the righteous,
> But You deliver the righteous out of them all.
>   (Psalm 34:18–19)

> You are my refuge and strength, O God,
> An ever-present help in trouble.
> Therefore I will not fear, though the earth changes
> And the mountains slip into the heart of the sea.
>   (Psalm 46:1–2)

Pause to offer your own expressions of thanksgiving.

Closing Prayer

> You, O Lord, are with me; I will not fear.
> What can people do to me?
> It is better to take refuge in You, Lord,
> Than to trust in people.
> It is better to take refuge in You
> Than to trust in princes. (Psalm 118:6, 8–9)

> I lift up my eyes to the hills—
> Where does my help come from?
> My help comes from You, O Lord,
> The One who made heaven and earth.
> You will not allow my foot to slip;

You, the One who watches over me, will not slumber.
You are my keeper;
You are my shade at my right hand.
The sun will not harm me by day,
Nor the moon by night. (Psalm 121:1–3, 5–6)

DAY 15

Adoration

> The works of Your hands, O Lord, are truth and justice;
> All Your precepts are trustworthy.
> They stand firm for ever and ever,
> Done in faithfulness and uprightness.
> You sent redemption to Your people;
> You have ordained Your covenant forever;
> Holy and awesome is Your name. (Psalm 111:7–9)

> Your name, O Lord, endures forever,
> Your renown, O Lord, through all generations.
>   (Psalm 135:13)

Pause to express your thoughts of praise and worship.

Confession

No temptation has overtaken me except what is common to all people. You are faithful; You will not let me be tempted beyond what I am able, but with the temptation, You will also provide a way out, so that I may be able to endure it. (1 Corinthians 10:13)

Ask the Spirit to search your heart and reveal any areas of unconfessed sin. Acknowledge these to the Lord and thank Him for His forgiveness.

Renewal

May I have no other gods before You. (Exodus 20:3; Deuteronomy 5:7)

May I not make for myself an idol in any form. (Exodus 20:4; Deuteronomy 5:8)

May I not take Your name, O Lord my God, in vain, for You will not hold anyone guiltless who misuses Your name. (Exodus 20:7; Deuteronomy 5:11)

Pause to add your own prayers for personal renewal.

Petition

Hear, O Lord, my voice when I call;
Be merciful to me and answer me.
My heart said of You, "Seek His face!"
Your face, Lord, I will seek. (Psalm 27:7–8)

Pause here to petition God for growth in love and compassion toward others. Offer prayers for your loved ones, for those who do not know Jesus and for those in need. Offer prayers regarding your activities for this day and any special concerns you may have.

Intercession

All things are for our benefit, so that the grace that is reaching more and more people may cause thanksgiving to abound to Your glory, O God. (2 Corinthians 4:15)

Take a few moments to intercede on behalf of friends, relatives, neighbors and coworkers who do not yet know salvation in Jesus Christ.

Affirmation

Is the law opposed to Your promises, O God? Certainly not! For if a law had been given that could impart life, then righteousness would indeed have been by the law. But the Scripture has declared all to be under sin, so that the promise by faith in Jesus Christ might be given to those who believe. (Galatians 3:21–22)

In You, O Christ, I was circumcised with a circumcision made without hands, in the removal of the body of sinful nature by Your circumcision, having been buried with You in baptism and raised with You through faith in the working of God, who raised You from the dead. (Colossians 2:11–12)

Pause to reflect on these Biblical affirmations.

Thanksgiving

We give thanks to You, O God, we give thanks,
For Your name is near;
We tell of Your wonderful works. (Psalm 75:1)

Lovingkindness and truth meet together;
Righteousness and peace kiss each other.
Truth springs forth from the earth,
And righteousness looks down from heaven.
    (Psalm 85:10–11)

Pause to offer your own expressions of thanksgiving.

Closing Prayer

O Lord, my heart is not proud, nor have my eyes been
    arrogant.
I do not concern myself with great matters
Or things too wonderful for me.
Surely I have stilled and quieted my soul;
Like a weaned child with its mother,
Like a weaned child is my soul within me.
    (Psalm 131:1–2)

DAY 16

Adoration

You, O Most High, are sovereign over the kingdoms of
all people
And give them to whomever You wish
And set over them the lowliest of people.
I will bless You, O Most High,
And praise and honor You, the One who lives forever.
Your dominion is an eternal dominion,
And Your kingdom endures from generation to
generation.
You regard all the inhabitants of the earth as nothing,
And do as You please with the host of heaven
And the inhabitants of the earth.
No one can hold back Your hand
Or say to You: "What have You done?"
I praise, exalt, and honor You, the King of heaven,
For all Your works are true, and all Your ways are just,
And You are able to humble those who walk in pride.
(Daniel 4:17, 34–35, 37)

Pause to express your thoughts of praise and worship.

Confession

You, Lord God, declared this assurance to Jeremiah: "I will
cleanse them from all of the sin they have committed against
Me, and I will forgive all of the sin they committed when
they turned away from Me." (Jeremiah 33:8)

*Ask the Spirit to search your heart and reveal any areas of
unconfessed sin. Acknowledge these to the Lord and thank Him
for His forgiveness.*

Renewal

May I honor my father and my mother. (Exodus 20:12; Deuteronomy 5:16)

May I not murder. (Exodus 20:13; Deuteronomy 5:17)

May I not commit adultery. (Exodus 20:14; Deuteronomy 5:18)

Pause to add your own prayers for personal renewal.

Petition

In You, O Lord, I have taken refuge;
Let me never be put to shame.
In Your righteousness deliver me and rescue me;
Turn Your ear to me and save me.
Be my rock of refuge, to which I can always go;
You have given the commandment to save me,
For You are my rock and my fortress. (Psalm 71:1–3)

Pause here to petition God to help you be a faithful steward of your time, talents, possessions and relationships. Offer prayers of petition regarding your activities for this day and any special concerns you may have.

Intercession

O Lord God of Israel, You are righteous, for we are left this day as a remnant. Here we are before You in our guilt, though no one can stand in Your presence because of it. (Ezra 9:15)

Take a few moments to intercede on behalf of your local, state or provincial, and national governments. Pray for spiritual revival in the nation and offer prayers regarding current events and concerns.

Affirmation

Your grace, O God, has appeared, bringing salvation to all people, teaching us to deny ungodliness and worldly passions and to live sensibly, righteously and godly in the present age. (Titus 2:11–12)

If I would love life and see good days, I must keep my tongue from evil and my lips from speaking guile. I must turn from evil and do good; I must seek peace and pursue it. For Your eyes, O Lord, are on the righteous, and Your ears attend to their prayer, but Your face is against those who do evil. (1 Peter 3:10–12)

Pause to reflect on these Biblical affirmations.

Thanksgiving

I will give thanks to You, Lord, for You are good;
Your lovingkindness endures forever.
I will give thanks to You for Your unfailing love
And Your wonderful acts to all Your people,
For You satisfy the thirsty soul
And fill the hungry soul with good things.
    (Psalm 107:1, 8–9)

Pause to offer your own expressions of thanksgiving.

Closing Prayer

You, the Lord my Redeemer, the Holy One of Israel
    have said:
"I am the Lord your God, who teaches you what is best
    for you,
Who leads you in the way you should go." (Isaiah 48:17)

Lord, You have said, "Come to Me, all you who labor and are heavy laden, and I will give you rest. Take My yoke upon you and learn from Me, for I am gentle and humble in heart, and you will find rest for your souls. For My yoke is easy, and My burden is light." (Matthew 11:28–30)

DAY 17

Adoration

O Christ, through You all things were made, and without You nothing was made that has been made. In You was life, and the life was our light. (John 1:3–4)

Lord Jesus, You are holy and true; You hold the key of David. What You open no one can shut, and what You shut no one can open. (Revelation 3:7)

Pause to express your thoughts of praise and worship.

Confession

> Let the wicked forsake their ways
> And the unrighteous their thoughts;
> Let them return to You, our Lord,
> And You will have mercy on them,
> And to You, our God, for You will abundantly pardon.
> (Isaiah 55:7)

Ask the Spirit to search your heart and reveal any areas of unconfessed sin. Acknowledge these to the Lord and thank Him for His forgiveness.

Renewal

May I not steal. (Exodus 20:15; Deuteronomy 5:19)

May I not bear false witness against my neighbor. (Exodus 20:16; Deuteronomy 5:20)

May I not covet my neighbor's house, my neighbor's wife, his manservant or maidservant, his ox or donkey, or anything that belongs to my neighbor. (Exodus 20:17; Deuteronomy 5:21)

Pause to add your own prayers for personal renewal.

Petition

> Out of the depths I call to You, O Lord.
> O Lord, hear my voice
> And let Your ears be attentive
> To the voice of my supplications. (Psalm 130:1–2)

Pause here to offer prayers of petition regarding your family and your ministry. Ask for His help and guidance in sharing Jesus with others and helping others grow in Him. Ask for guidance in your vocation and your avocations. Offer prayers of petition regarding your activities for this day and any special concerns you may have.

Intercession

Holy Spirit, You convict the world concerning sin and righteousness and judgment. (John 16:8)

Take a few moments to intercede on behalf of local, national and world missions. Pray that the Great Commission would be fulfilled and for any special concerns you may have for missions.

Affirmation

Those who are wise and understanding will show it by their good conduct and works done in the humility that comes from wisdom. If I harbor bitter envy and selfish ambition in my heart, I should not boast and lie against the truth. This kind of wisdom does not come down from above, but is earthly, natural, demonic. For where there is envy and selfish ambition, there is disorder and every evil practice. (James 3:13–16)

The wisdom that comes from above is first pure, then peaceable, gentle, submissive, full of mercy and good fruits, without partiality and hypocrisy. And the fruit of righteousness is sown in peace by those who make peace. (James 3:17–18)

Pause to reflect on these Biblical affirmations.

Thanksgiving

I give thanks for the word of Your angels to the shepherds: "Do not be afraid. I bring you good news of great joy that will be for all the people. For today in the city of David a Savior has been born to you, who is Christ the Lord." (Luke 2:10–11)

You, Jesus, the Son of Man, came to seek and to save that which was lost. (Luke 19:10)

We give You thanks that to all who receive You, Lord Jesus Christ, and believe in Your name, You give the right to become children of God—children born not of natural descent, nor of human decision or a husband's will, but born of God. (John 1:12–13)

Pause to offer your own expressions of thanksgiving.

Closing Prayer

If I wish to come after You, I must deny myself and take up my cross and follow You. For if I want to save my life, I will lose it, but if I lose my life for You and for the gospel, I will find it. For what profit will I have if I gain the whole world, yet forfeit my soul? Or what will I give in exchange for my soul? (Matthew 16:24–26; Mark 8:34–37; Luke 9:23–25)

I shall know the truth, and the truth shall set me free. Everyone who commits sin is a slave of sin. And a slave has no permanent place in the family, but a child belongs to it forever. So if You, the Son of God, set me free, I shall be free indeed. (John 8:32, 34–36)

DAY 18

Adoration

> We praise You, Lord!
> We give thanks to You, for You are good;
> For Your loving mercy endures forever.
> Who can express Your mighty acts, O Lord,
> Or fully declare Your praise? (Psalm 106:1–2)
>
> You endowed the heart with wisdom
> And gave understanding to the mind. (Job 38:36)

Pause to express your thoughts of praise and worship.

Confession

> Search me, O God, and know my heart;
> Try me and know my anxious thoughts.
> See if there is any wicked way in me,
> And lead me in the way everlasting. (Psalm 139:23–24)

Ask the Spirit to search your heart and reveal any areas of unconfessed sin. Acknowledge these to the Lord and thank Him for His forgiveness.

Renewal

Lord, may these beatitudes become a reality in my life:

Blessed are the poor in spirit, for theirs is the kingdom of heaven. Blessed are those who mourn, for they will be comforted. Blessed are the meek, for they will inherit the earth. (Matthew 5:3–5)

Blessed are those who hunger and thirst for righteousness, for they shall be satisfied. (Matthew 5:6)

Blessed are the merciful, for they shall obtain mercy. (Matthew 5:7)

Pause to add your own prayers for personal renewal.

Petition

May I not wear myself out to get rich;
Give me the understanding to cease.
May I not set my desire on what flies away,
For wealth surely sprouts wings
And flies into the heavens like an eagle. (Proverbs 23:4–5)

Pause here to petition God for growth in your character and personal discipline, and for physical health and strength. Ask that He empower you for spiritual warfare against the temptations of the world, the flesh and the devil. Offer prayers regarding your activities for this day and any special concerns you may have.

Intercession

May I learn to do good,
Seek justice,
Remove the oppressor,
Defend the orphan,
And plead for the widow. (Isaiah 1:17)

Take a few moments to intercede on behalf of the poor and hungry, the oppressed and persecuted, and those in control of world and national resources. Offer prayers for peace among nations and regarding current events and concerns.

Affirmation

Lord Jesus, those who love You will keep Your word; and Your Father will love them, and You and Your Father will come to them and make Your home with them. (John 14:23)

If I serve You, I must follow You; and where You are, I also will be. If I serve You, the Father will honor me. (John 12:26)

Pause to reflect on these Biblical affirmations.

Thanksgiving

> Blessed is the one You choose and bring near
> To live in Your courts.
> I will be satisfied with the goodness of Your house,
> Of Your holy temple. (Psalm 65:4)

> He who rests in Your shadow, O Most High God,
> Will be kept safe by You, O Mighty One.
> I will say of You, "You are my refuge and my fortress, O Lord;
> You are God, in whom I trust." (Psalm 91:1–2)

Pause to offer your own expressions of thanksgiving.

Closing Prayer

Lord, You are the One who gives endurance and encouragement; grant that we be of the same mind toward one another, according to Christ Jesus, so that with one accord and one mouth we may glorify You, the God and Father of our Lord Jesus Christ. (Romans 15:5–6)

May You, the God of peace, sanctify us completely, and may our whole spirit, soul and body be preserved blameless at the coming of our Lord Jesus Christ. You, the One who calls us, are faithful; You also will do it. (1 Thessalonians 5:23–24)

Adoration

O Lord, we worship You and Your Son Jesus,
for You have made Him our Messiah and King:

> His throne is Your very throne, O God.
> His kingdom will last for ever and ever.
> He will rule by treating everyone fairly.
> He loves what is right and hates what is evil.
> So You have placed Him above His companions.
> You have filled Him with joy by pouring the sacred oil
> on His head. (Psalm 45:6–7)

> One generation shall praise Your works to another,
> And shall declare Your mighty acts.
> I will meditate on the glorious splendor of Your majesty
> And on Your wonderful works.
> Many shall speak of the might of Your awesome works,
> And I will proclaim Your great deeds. (Psalm 145:4–6)

Pause to express your thoughts of praise and worship.

Confession

> Purge me with hyssop, and I will be clean;
> Wash me, and I will be whiter than snow.
> Cause me to hear joy and gladness,
> That the bones You have crushed may rejoice.
> Hide Your face from my sins
> And blot out all my iniquities.
> Create in me a clean heart, O God,
> And renew a steadfast spirit within me.
> Do not cast me from Your presence
> Or take Your Holy Spirit from me.

Restore to me the joy of Your salvation
And uphold me with a willing spirit.
Then I will teach transgressors Your ways,
And sinners will be converted to You. (Psalm 51:7–13)

Ask the Spirit to search your heart and reveal any areas of unconfessed sin. Acknowledge these to the Lord and thank Him for His forgiveness.

Renewal

Lord, may Your beatitudes become a reality in my life:

Blessed are the pure in heart, for they shall see God. Blessed are the peacemakers, for they shall be called children of God. (Matthew 5:8–9)

Blessed are those who are persecuted for the sake of righteousness, for theirs is the kingdom of heaven. Blessed are you when people insult you, persecute you, and falsely say all kinds of evil against you because of Me. Rejoice and be glad, because great is your reward in heaven, for in the same way they persecuted the prophets who were before you. (Matthew 5:10–12)

Pause to add your own prayers for personal renewal.

Petition

I called on Your name, O Lord,
From the depths of the pit.
You have heard my voice:
"Do not hide Your ear from my cry for relief,
From my cry for help."
You drew near when I called on You,
And You said, "Do not fear!"
O Lord, You pleaded the cause of my soul;
You redeemed my life. (Lamentations 3:55–58)

Pause here to petition God for growth in your desire to know and please Jesus Christ. Pray for a greater love and commitment to Him, for the grace to practice His presence and for the grace to glorify Him in your life. Offer prayers regarding your activities for this day and any special concerns you may have.

Intercession

We were all baptized by one Spirit into one body—whether Jews or Greeks, slave or free—and we were all given the one Spirit to drink. (1 Corinthians 12:13)

Take a few moments to intercede on behalf of your local church, other churches, evangelism and discipleship ministries, educational ministries and any other special concerns you may have.

Affirmation

Surely Your salvation is near to those who fear You.
   (Psalm 85:9)

To fear You, O Lord, is the beginning of knowledge,
But fools despise wisdom and discipline. (Proverbs 1:7)

To fear You, O Lord, is a fountain of life,
Turning one away from the snares of death.
   (Proverbs 14:27)

Your secrets are with those who fear You, O Lord,
And You will make them know Your covenant.
   (Psalm 25:14)

Pause to reflect on these Biblical affirmations.

Thanksgiving

Surely the righteous will give thanks to Your name;
The upright will dwell in Your presence. (Psalm 140:13)

O Lord, You are near to all who call upon You,
To all who call upon You in truth.
You fulfill the desire of those who fear You;
You hear their cry and save them.
You preserve all who love You,
But all the wicked You will destroy. (Psalm 145:18–20)

Pause to offer your own expressions of thanksgiving.

Closing Prayer

By common confession, great is the mystery of
    godliness:
You, Jesus Christ, who were revealed in the flesh,
Vindicated in the Spirit,
Seen by angels,
Preached among the nations,
Believed on in the world,
Taken up in glory. (1 Timothy 3:16)

DAY 20

Adoration

I will regard You as holy, Lord of hosts;
You shall be my fear,
And You shall be my dread. (Isaiah 8:13)

You are the stability of our times,
A wealth of salvation, wisdom and knowledge.
Fearing You, O Lord, is the key to this treasure.
(Isaiah 33:6)

Pause to express your thoughts of praise and worship.

Confession

I will sing praises to You, O Lord,
And give thanks at the remembrance of Your holy name.
For Your anger lasts only a moment,
But Your favor is for a lifetime;
Weeping may endure for a night,
But joy comes in the morning. (Psalm 30:4–5)

Ask the Spirit to search your heart and reveal any areas of unconfessed sin. Acknowledge these to the Lord and thank Him for His forgiveness.

Renewal

May I be righteous before You, O God, walking blamelessly in all Your commandments and ordinances. (Luke 1:6)

May I love my enemies, do good to those who hate me, bless those who curse me, and pray for those who mistreat me. May I do to others as I would have them do to me. (Luke 6:27–28, 31)

Pause to add your own prayers for personal renewal.

Petition

I look to You for my daily bread, to forgive me my debts as I also have forgiven my debtors. Do not lead me into temptation, but deliver me from the evil one. For Yours is the kingdom and the power and the glory forever. (Matthew 6:11–13)

Pause here to petition God for wisdom. Ask Him to develop your eternal perspective, to renew your mind with truth and to help you develop greater skill in each area of your life. Offer prayers regarding your activities for this day and any special concerns you may have.

Intercession

Oh, that we would always have such a heart to fear You and keep all Your commandments, so that it might be well with us and with our children forever! (Deuteronomy 5:29)

Take a few moments to intercede on behalf of your immediate family and other relatives. Offer prayers for their spiritual, emotional and physical concerns.

Affirmation

I know that whatever You do, O God, will remain forever; nothing can be added to it and nothing taken from it. You do it so that people will revere You. (Ecclesiastes 3:14)

You, O God, will bring every work into judgment, including every hidden thing, whether it is good or evil. (Ecclesiastes 12:14)

Pause to reflect on these Biblical affirmations.

Thanksgiving

Because I love You, You will deliver me;
You will protect me, for I acknowledge Your name.
I will call upon You, and You will answer me;
You will be with me in trouble,
You will deliver me and honor me.
With long life You will satisfy me
And show me Your salvation. (Psalm 91:14–16)

Pause to offer your own expressions of thanksgiving.

Closing Prayer

Your word, O God, is living and active and sharper than any double-edged sword, piercing even to the dividing of soul and spirit and of joints and marrow, and it judges the thoughts and attitudes of the heart. And there is no creature hidden from Your sight, but everything is uncovered and laid bare before Your eyes; to You we must give account. (Hebrews 4:12–13)

Being built up in the most holy faith and praying in the Holy Spirit, may I keep myself in Your love, O God, as I wait for the mercy of our Lord Jesus Christ to bring me eternal life. (Jude 20–21)

DAY 21

Adoration

O Lord, You made the earth by Your power;
You established the world by Your wisdom
And stretched out the heavens by Your understanding.
    (Jeremiah 10:12; 51:15)

You give the sun for light by day, O Lord,
And decree the moon and stars for light by night;
You stir up the sea so that its waves roar;
The Lord of hosts is Your name. (Jeremiah 31:35)

Pause to express your thoughts of praise and worship.

Confession

O Lord, God of heaven, You are the great and awesome God, keeping Your covenant of loyal love with those who love You and obey Your commands. Let Your ear be attentive and Your eyes open so that You may hear the prayer Your servant is praying before You day and night. I confess the sins I have committed against You. (Nehemiah 1:5–6)

Ask the Spirit to search your heart and reveal any areas of unconfessed sin. Acknowledge these to the Lord and thank Him for His forgiveness.

Renewal

Just as I once presented the parts of my body as slaves to impurity and to ever-increasing lawlessness, so I now present them as slaves to righteousness, leading to holiness. (Romans 6:19)

Those who live according to the flesh set their minds on the things of the flesh; but those who live according to Your Spirit,

O God, set their minds on the things of the Spirit. The mind of the flesh is death, but the mind of Your Spirit is life and peace. (Romans 8:5–6)

Pause to add your own prayers for personal renewal.

Petition

May I watch carefully how I walk, not as unwise but as wise, making the most of every opportunity, because the days are evil. May I not be foolish, but understand what Your will is, O Lord. (Ephesians 5:15–17)

Pause here to petition God for spiritual insight so that you might have understanding of His Word. Ask for insight into your identity in Jesus Christ: that you might know who you are, what direction your life should take and what His purpose for your life is. Offer prayers regarding your activities for this day and any special concerns you may have.

Intercession

May we always thank You, O God, for other believers and pray that their faith would grow more and more, and that their love for each other would increase. (2 Thessalonians 1:3)

Take a few moments to intercede on behalf of other believers, such as your personal friends, those in ministry and those who are oppressed and in need.

Affirmation

> All people are like grass, and all their glory is like the flower of the field.
> The grass withers and the flower fades,
> Because Your breath, Lord, blows on it.
> Surely the people are like grass.

The grass withers and the flower fades,
But Your word stands forever. (Isaiah 40:6–8)

Heaven and earth will pass away, but Your words, Lord Jesus,
will never pass away. (Matthew 24:35; Luke 21:33)

Pause to reflect on these Biblical affirmations.

Thanksgiving

Surely You are my salvation, O God;
I will trust and not be afraid.
For You are my strength and my song,
And You have become my salvation. (Isaiah 12:2)

I will trust in You, O Lord, forever,
For in You, the Lord, I have an everlasting Rock.
(Isaiah 26:4)

Pause to offer your own expressions of thanksgiving.

Closing Prayer

Your eyes, O Lord, move to and fro throughout the whole
earth to strengthen those whose hearts are fully committed
to You. (2 Chronicles 16:9)

I have set You, Lord, always before me.
Because You are at my right hand, I will not be shaken.
Therefore my heart is glad, and my glory rejoices;
My body also will rest in hope.
You will make known to me the path of life;
In Your presence is fullness of joy;
In Your right hand are pleasures forever.
(Psalm 16:8–9, 11)

DAY 22

Adoration

O Lord, the God of our fathers, are You not the God who is in heaven? Are You not the ruler over all the kingdoms of the nations? Power and might are in Your hand, and no one is able to withstand You. (2 Chronicles 20:6)

> I will praise You, O Lord, with all my heart;
> I will tell of all Your wonders.
> I will be glad and rejoice in You;
> I will sing praise to Your name, O Most High.
>   (Psalm 9:1–2)

Pause to express your thoughts of praise and worship.

Confession

> Have You as much delight in burnt offerings and
>   sacrifices, O Lord,
> As in obedience to Your voice?
> To obey is better than sacrifice,
> And to heed is better than the fat of rams.
> For rebellion is like the sin of divination,
> And stubbornness is as iniquity and idolatry.
>   (1 Samuel 15:22–23)

Ask the Spirit to search your heart and reveal any areas of unconfessed sin. Acknowledge these to the Lord and thank Him for His forgiveness.

Renewal

May I put away all bitterness and anger and wrath and shouting and slander, along with all malice. And may I be kind and compassionate to others, forgiving them just as You, O God, in Christ also forgave me. (Ephesians 4:31–32)

May I do all things without complaining or arguing, so that I may become blameless and pure—Your child, O God, without fault in the midst of a crooked and perverse generation, among whom I shine as a light in the world, holding out the word of life. (Philippians 2:14–16)

Pause to add your own prayers for personal renewal.

Petition

As one of Your chosen people, holy and beloved, may I put on a heart of compassion, kindness, humility, gentleness and patience, bearing with others and forgiving others even as You, Lord, forgave me; and above all these things may I put on love, which is the bond of perfection. (Colossians 3:12–14)

Pause here to petition God for growth in love and compassion toward others. Offer prayers for your loved ones, for those who do not know Jesus and for those in need. Offer prayers regarding your activities for this day and any special concerns you may have.

Intercession

Jesus, You say to us: "Behold . . . lift up your eyes and look at the fields, for they are white for harvest. Even now the reaper draws his wages, and gathers fruit for eternal life, that those who sow and those who reap may rejoice together." (John 4:35–36)

Take a few moments to intercede on behalf of friends, relatives, neighbors and coworkers who do not yet know salvation in Jesus Christ.

Affirmation

Whoever is faithful with very little is also faithful with much, and whoever is dishonest with very little will also be dishonest with much. If I am not faithful in handling worldly wealth, who will trust me with true riches? And if I am not faithful with someone else's property, who will give me property of my own? (Luke 16:10–12)

This is a trustworthy saying: If we died with You, we will also live with You; if we endure, we will also reign with You. If we deny You, You will also deny us; if we are faithless, You will remain faithful, for You cannot deny Yourself. (2 Timothy 2:11–13)

Pause to reflect on these Biblical affirmations.

Thanksgiving

You, O Lord, will bare Your holy arm
In the sight of all the nations,
And all the ends of the earth will see
Your salvation. (Isaiah 52:10)

You, O Lord, have performed mighty deeds with Your arm;
You have scattered those who are proud in the thoughts of their hearts.
You have brought down rulers from their thrones
And have lifted up the humble. (Luke 1:51–52)

Pause to offer your own expressions of thanksgiving.

Closing Prayer

You, O God, are the maker of the Bear and Orion, the Pleiades,
And the constellations of the south.

You do great things that cannot be fathomed
And wonderful works that cannot be counted.
   (Job 9:9–10)

When I consider Your heavens, the work of Your
   fingers,
The moon and the stars, which You have set in place,
What is a human being that You are mindful of him,
And the son of man that You care for him?
You made him a little lower than the heavenly beings
And crowned him with glory and honor.
You made human beings the rulers over the works of
   Your hands,
And You put everything under their feet. (Psalm 8:3–6)

Adoration

> The righteous will rejoice in You, O Lord;
> Praise is becoming to the upright. (Psalm 33:1)

> Walking in the way of Your laws,
> O Lord, I wait for You;
> Your name and Your memory are the desire of my soul.
>   (Isaiah 26:8)

Pause to express your thoughts of praise and worship.

Confession

> Woe to me, for I am undone!
> Because I have unclean lips,
> And I live among a people of unclean lips,
> And my eyes have seen You, the King,
> The Lord of hosts. (Isaiah 6:5)

Ask the Spirit to search your heart and reveal any areas of unconfessed sin. Acknowledge these to the Lord and thank Him for His forgiveness.

Renewal

If I have found grace in Your sight, teach me Your ways, so I may know You and continue to find favor with You. (Exodus 33:13)

May I consecrate myself and be holy, because You are the Lord my God. May I keep Your statutes and practice them, for You are the Lord who sanctifies me. (Leviticus 20:7–8)

Pause to add your own prayers for personal renewal.

Petition

May I examine all things, hold fast to the good, and abstain from every form of evil. (1 Thessalonians 5:21–22)

Pause here to petition God to help you be a faithful steward of your time, talents, possessions and relationships. Offer prayers of petition regarding your activities for this day and any special concerns you may have.

Intercession

O Lord, God of our fathers Abraham, Isaac and Israel, keep this desire in the hearts of Your people forever, and keep their hearts loyal to You. (1 Chronicles 29:18)

Take a few moments to intercede on behalf of your local, state or provincial, and national governments. Pray for spiritual revival in the nation and offer prayers regarding current events and concerns.

Affirmation

Where is the wise person? Where is the scholar? Where is the disputer of this age? O God, have You not made foolish the wisdom of the world? But to those whom You have called, both Jews and Greeks, Christ is Your power and Your wisdom. (1 Corinthians 1:20, 24)

If I think I am somebody when I am nobody, I am fooling myself. (Galatians 6:3)

Let those who boast, boast in You, Lord. (1 Corinthians 1:31)

Pause to reflect on these Biblical affirmations.

Thanksgiving

Jesus, we give thanks that You expressed Your concern for the lost when You said, "What man among you, if he has a hundred sheep and loses one of them, does not leave the ninety-nine in the open country and go after the one that is lost until he finds it? And when he finds it, he lays it on his shoulders, rejoicing. And when he comes into his house, he calls his friends and neighbors together and says to them, 'Rejoice with me, for I have found my sheep which was lost!' I tell you that, in the same way, there will be more joy in heaven over one sinner who repents than over ninety-nine righteous people who need no repentance. There is joy in the presence of the angels of God over one sinner who repents." (Luke 15:4–7, 10)

Pause to offer your own expressions of thanksgiving.

Closing Prayer

Now I know that You save Your anointed, O Lord;
You answer from Your holy heaven
With the saving strength of Your right hand.
Some trust in chariots and some in horses,
But I will remember Your name, O Lord my God.
   (Psalm 20:6–7)

May all Your saints love You, O Lord!
You preserve the faithful
And fully repay the proud.
We will be of good courage
For You will strengthen the hearts of those who hope in
   You. (Psalm 31:23–24)

DAY 24

Adoration

You, O Lord, have declared:
"My thoughts are not your thoughts,
Neither are your ways My ways.
As the heavens are higher than the earth,
So are My ways higher than your ways,
And My thoughts than your thoughts." (Isaiah 55:8–9)

You are the Lord, the God of all humankind. Nothing is too difficult for You. (Jeremiah 32:27)

Pause to express your thoughts of praise and worship.

Confession

The heart is deceitful above all things
And incurably sick.
Who can understand it?
You, Lord, search people's hearts
And test people's minds
To reward them according to their ways,
According to the fruit of their deeds. (Jeremiah 17:9–10)

Ask the Spirit to search your heart and reveal any areas of unconfessed sin. Acknowledge these to the Lord and thank Him for His forgiveness.

Renewal

May I not profane Your holy name, but acknowledge You as holy before others. You are the Lord who sanctifies me. (Leviticus 22:32)

You, the Lord my God, are one Lord. May I love You with all my heart and with all my soul and with all my strength. (Deuteronomy 6:4–5)

Pause to add your own prayers for personal renewal.

Petition

May I fight the good fight, finish the race, and keep the faith, so that there will be laid up for me the crown of righteousness, which You, Lord, the righteous Judge, will award to me on that day; and not only to me, but also to all who have longed for Christ's appearing. (2 Timothy 4:7–8)

Pause here to offer prayers of petition regarding your family and your ministry. Ask for help and guidance in sharing Jesus with others and helping others grow in Him. Ask for guidance in your vocation and your avocations. Offer prayers of petition regarding your activities for this day and any special concerns you may have.

Intercession

You, Lord Jesus, told the apostles, "You will receive power when the Holy Spirit comes upon you; and you will be My witnesses in Jerusalem, and in all Judea and Samaria, and to the ends of the earth." (Acts 1:8)

Take a few moments to intercede on behalf of local, national and world missions. Pray that the Great Commission would be fulfilled and for any special concerns you may have for missions.

Affirmation

> Whoever is wise understands these things;
> Whoever is discerning knows them.
> Your ways, O Lord, are right;
> The righteous will walk in them,
> But transgressors will stumble in them. (Hosea 14:9)

You have called the humble of the earth to seek You, O Lord, and those who have upheld Your justice to seek righteousness and humility. (Zephaniah 2:3)

Pause to reflect on these Biblical affirmations.

Thanksgiving

You sent Your word to the children of Israel, O God, telling the good news of peace through Jesus Christ, who is Lord of all. Jesus commanded the apostles to preach to the people and to testify that He is the One whom You appointed as judge of the living and the dead. To Him all the prophets witness that through His name, everyone who believes in Him receives forgiveness of sins. (Acts 10:36, 42–43)

You have loved me and called me to be a saint; You, Father, and the Lord Jesus Christ have given me grace and peace. (Romans 1:7)

Pause to offer your own expressions of thanksgiving.

Closing Prayer

Why is my soul downcast?
Why am I disturbed deep within my being?
I will hope in You, O God; I will yet praise You
For the help of Your presence.
O my God, my soul is downcast within me;
Therefore I will remember You.
Why is my soul downcast?
Why am I disturbed deep within my being?
I will hope in You, O God; I will yet praise You,
The help of my countenance and my God.
  (Psalm 42:5–6, 11)

DAY 25

Adoration

Thrones were set in place,
And You, O Ancient of Days, took Your seat.
Your clothing was as white as snow,
And the hair of Your head was like pure wool.
Your throne was ablaze with flames,
And its wheels were a burning fire.
A river of fire was flowing
And coming out from before You.
A thousand thousands attended You;
Ten thousand times ten thousand stood before You.
The court was seated,
And the books were opened. (Daniel 7:9–10)

O Lord, God of Israel, enthroned between the cherubim,
You alone are God over all the kingdoms of the earth. You
have made heaven and earth. (2 Kings 19:15)

Pause to express your thoughts of praise and worship.

Confession

You, O Lord, have declared, "Even now
Return to Me with all your heart,
With fasting and weeping and mourning.
So rend your heart and not your garments."
We will return to You, O Lord our God,
For You are gracious and compassionate,
Slow to anger and abounding in lovingkindness,
And You relent from sending calamity. (Joel 2:12–13)

*Ask the Spirit to search your heart and reveal any areas of
unconfessed sin. Acknowledge these to the Lord and thank Him
for His forgiveness.*

Renewal

> May I preserve sound wisdom and discretion,
> Not letting them out of my sight;
> They will be life to my soul. (Proverbs 3:21–22)

May I not let Your Word depart from my mouth, but meditate on it day and night, so that I may be careful to do all that is written in it; for then I will be prosperous, and I will act wisely. (Joshua 1:8)

Pause to add your own prayers for personal renewal.

Petition

By Your grace, O God, I want to live to the end in faith, knowing that I will not receive the promises on earth; I see them and welcome them from a distance. I confess that I am a stranger and a pilgrim on the earth. I long for a better country, a heavenly one. In this way, You will not be ashamed to be called my God, for You have prepared a city for me. Like Moses, may I esteem reproach for the sake of Christ as of greater value than the treasures of this world, because I am looking to the reward. (Hebrews 11:13, 16, 26)

Pause here to petition God for growth in your character and personal discipline, and for physical health and strength. Ask that He empower you for spiritual warfare against the temptations of the world, the flesh and the devil. Offer prayers regarding your activities for this day and any special concerns you may have.

Intercession

Hear from heaven, Your dwelling place, and forgive us and deal with each of us according to what we do, since You know our hearts (for You alone know people's hearts). (2 Chronicles 6:30)

Take a few moments to intercede on behalf of the poor and hungry, the oppressed and persecuted, and those in control of world and national resources. Offer prayers for peace among nations and regarding current events and concerns.

Affirmation

From the rising of the sun to its setting, Your name will be great among the nations. In every place incense and pure offerings will be brought to Your name, for Your name will be great among the nations. (Malachi 1:11)

All authority in heaven and on earth has been given to You, Jesus Christ, who are the Son of God. (Matthew 28:18)

Lord Jesus Christ, you are coming with the clouds, and every eye will see You, even those who pierced You; and all the peoples of the earth will mourn because of You. Even so, Amen. (Revelation 1:7)

Pause to reflect on these Biblical affirmations.

Thanksgiving

> The salvation of the righteous comes from You, Lord;
> You are their stronghold in time of trouble.
> You help them and deliver them;
> You deliver them from the wicked and save them,
> Because they take refuge in You. (Psalm 37:39–40)

Pause to offer your own expressions of thanksgiving.

Closing Prayer

> Be exalted, O God, above the heavens;
> Let Your glory be over all the earth.
> I will praise You, O Lord, among the peoples;
> I will sing to You among the nations.

For Your mercy reaches to the heavens,
And Your faithfulness reaches to the clouds.
Be exalted, O God, above the heavens;
Let Your glory be above all the earth. (Psalm 57:5, 9–11)

DAY 26

Adoration

Behold, You who form the mountains and create the
    wind,
And reveal Your thoughts to people;
You turn dawn to darkness,
And tread the high places of the earth—
The Lord God of hosts is Your name. (Amos 4:13)

In Your majesty, You dwell in the likeness of a throne of sapphire above the expanse that is over the cherubim. (Ezekiel 10:1)

Pause to express your thoughts of praise and worship.

Confession

Our fathers disciplined us for a little while as they thought best, but You, O God, discipline us for our good, that we may share in Your holiness. No discipline seems pleasant at the time, but painful; later on, however, it produces the peaceable fruit of righteousness for those who have been trained by it. Therefore, let us strengthen our hands that are weary and our feeble knees, and make straight paths for our feet, so that what is lame may not be disabled, but rather healed. (Hebrews 12:10–13)

Ask the Spirit to search your heart and reveal any areas of unconfessed sin. Acknowledge these to the Lord and thank Him for His forgiveness.

Renewal

May I not be afraid of those who kill the body and after that can do no more. But I will fear You, the One who, after killing, has authority to cast into hell. (Luke 12:4–5)

May I fear only You, O Lord my God, and serve You and take my oaths in Your name. (Deuteronomy 6:13)

May I be very careful to love You, O Lord my God, to walk in all Your ways, to obey Your commands, to hold fast to You, and to serve You with all my heart and all my soul. (Joshua 22:5)

Pause to add your own prayers for personal renewal.

Petition

May I submit myself for Your sake, O Lord, to every human authority, whether to a king as being supreme, or to governors sent by him to punish evildoers and to praise those who do right; for it is Your will that by doing good I may silence the ignorance of foolish men. (1 Peter 2:13–15)

Pause here to petition God for growth in your desire to know and please Jesus Christ. Pray for a greater love and commitment to Him, for the grace to practice His presence and for the grace to glorify Him in your life. Offer prayers regarding your activities for this day and any special concerns you may have.

Intercession

We should not get drunk on wine, for that is dissipation. Instead, we should be filled with Your Spirit, speaking to one another with psalms, hymns, and spiritual songs; singing and making music in our hearts to You, always giving thanks to You for everything, God our Father, in the name of our Lord Jesus Christ. (Ephesians 5:18–20)

Take a few moments to intercede on behalf of your local church, other churches, evangelism and discipleship ministries, educational ministries and any other special concerns you may have.

Affirmation

Lord Jesus, You have said that unless I am converted and become like a little child, I will never enter the kingdom of heaven. Therefore, those who humble themselves like children are the greatest in the kingdom of heaven. (Matthew 18:3–4)

Let us not hinder the little children from coming to You, Lord Jesus, for of such is the kingdom of heaven. (Matthew 19:14)

Pause to reflect on these Biblical affirmations.

Thanksgiving

We praise You, Lord; day by day You bear our burdens,
O God of our salvation.
You, our God, are the God of salvation,
And to You belongs escape from death. (Psalm 68:19–20)

It is good to give thanks to You, O Lord,
And to sing praises to Your name, O Most High,
To declare Your lovingkindness in the morning
And Your faithfulness at night. (Psalm 92:1–2)

Pause to offer your own expressions of thanksgiving.

Closing Prayer

I remember You on my bed, O Lord,
And I meditate on You through the watches of the night.
Because You have been my help,
I will rejoice in the shadow of Your wings.
My soul clings to You;
Your right hand upholds me. (Psalm 63:6–8)

DAY 27

Adoration

Heaven is Your throne,
And the earth is Your footstool.
Your hand made all these things,
And so they came into being. (Isaiah 66:1–2)

Your hand laid the foundations of the earth,
And Your right hand spread out the heavens;
When You summon them, they all stand up together.
(Isaiah 48:13)

Pause to express your thoughts of praise and worship.

Confession

Surely You desire truth in the inner parts,
And in the hidden part You make me know wisdom.
(Psalm 51:6)

Ask the Spirit to search your heart and reveal any areas of unconfessed sin. Acknowledge these to the Lord and thank Him for His forgiveness.

Renewal

Like Josiah, may I do what is right in Your sight, O Lord, and walk in all the ways of David, not turning aside to the right or to the left. May I turn to You with all my heart and with all my soul and with all my might, in accordance with all of Your Word. (2 Kings 22:1–2; 23:25)

May I speak the truth to others and judge with truth and justice. May I not plot evil against my neighbor nor love a false oath; for all these things You hate, O Lord. (Zechariah 8:16–17)

Pause to add your own prayers for personal renewal.

Petition

May I not be afraid of my adversaries, but remember You, the One who is great and awesome. (Nehemiah 4:14)

Pause here to petition God for wisdom. Ask Him to develop your eternal perspective, to renew your mind with truth and to help you develop greater skill in each area of your life. Offer prayers regarding your activities for this day and any special concerns you may have.

Intercession

May I do nothing out of selfish ambition or vain conceit, but in humility may I esteem others as more important than myself. Let me look not only to my own interests, but also to the interests of others. (Philippians 2:3–4)

Take a few moments to intercede on behalf of your immediate family and other relatives. Offer prayers for their spiritual, emotional and physical concerns.

Affirmation

You, Jesus, will be great and will be called the Son of the Most High. The Lord God will give You the throne of Your father David, and You will reign over the house of Jacob forever, and Your kingdom will never end. (Luke 1:32–33)

> The heavens will vanish like smoke;
> The earth will wear out like a garment,
> And its inhabitants will die in the same way.
> But Your salvation will last forever,
> And Your righteousness will never fail. (Isaiah 51:6)

You were pleased, O God, to have all Your fullness dwell in Christ and through Him to reconcile all things to Yourself, whether things on earth or things in heaven, having made peace through the blood of His cross. (Colossians 1:19–20)

Pause to reflect on these Biblical affirmations.

Thanksgiving

Let those who love You, O Lord, hate evil.
You preserve the souls of Your saints
And deliver them from the hand of the wicked.
Light is sown for the righteous
And gladness for the upright in heart.
    (Psalm 97:10–11)

Pause to offer your own expressions of thanksgiving.

Closing Prayer

You, O Lord, have established Your throne in heaven,
And Your kingdom rules over all.
May all Your angels bless You, Lord,
Your angels who are mighty and do Your bidding,
Obeying the voice of Your word.
May all Your hosts bless You, Lord,
Your servants who do Your will.
May all Your works bless You, Lord,
In all places of Your dominion.
May my soul bless You, O Lord. (Psalm 103:19–22)

Adoration

We praise You, the God and Father of our Lord Jesus Christ, for You have blessed us with every spiritual blessing in the heavenly realms in Christ. (Ephesians 1:3)

Lord Jesus Christ, You gave Yourself for our sins to rescue us from the present evil age, according to the will of our God and Father, to whom be glory for ever and ever. (Galatians 1:3–5)

Pause to express your thoughts of praise and worship.

Confession

Blessed is the one whose transgression is forgiven,
Whose sin is covered.
Blessed is the one to whom You, O Lord, do not
impute iniquity
And in whose spirit is no deceit.
When I kept silent, my bones wasted away
Through my groaning all day long.
For day and night Your hand was heavy upon me;
My strength was sapped as in the heat of summer.
I acknowledged my sin to You
And did not hide my iniquity.
I said, "I will confess my transgressions to the Lord,"
And You forgave the guilt of my sin. (Psalm 32:1–5)

Ask the Spirit to search your heart and reveal any areas of unconfessed sin. Acknowledge these to the Lord and thank Him for His forgiveness.

Renewal

May I take heed not to practice my righteousness before people, to be seen by them. Otherwise, I will have no reward from You, my Father in heaven. (Matthew 6:1)

May I not fear those who kill the body but cannot kill the soul, but rather may I fear You, the One who is able to destroy both soul and body in hell. (Matthew 10:28)

Pause to add your own prayers for personal renewal.

Petition

In You, O Lord, I have taken refuge;
Let me never be ashamed;
Deliver me in Your righteousness.
Since You are my rock and my fortress,
For Your name's sake lead me and guide me.
Into Your hands I commit my spirit;
Redeem me, O Lord God of truth. (Psalm 31:1, 3, 5)

Pause here to petition God for spiritual insight so that you might have understanding of His Word. Ask for insight into your identity in Jesus Christ: that you might know who you are, what direction your life should take and what His purpose for your life is. Offer prayers regarding your activities for this day and any special concerns you may have.

Intercession

Jesus, You have given us a new commandment: to love one another even as You have loved us, so we must love one another. By this all people will know that we are Your disciples, if we have love for one another. (John 13:34)

Take a few moments to intercede on behalf of other believers, such as your personal friends, those in ministry and those who are oppressed and in need.

Affirmation

Multitudes who sleep in the dust of the earth will awake, some to everlasting life, others to shame and everlasting contempt. Those who are wise will shine like the brightness of the heavens, and those who lead many to righteousness will be like the stars for ever and ever. (Daniel 12:2–3)

An hour is coming when all who are in the graves will hear Your voice, O Son of Man, and will come out—those who have done good will rise to a resurrection of life, and those who have done evil will rise to a resurrection of judgment. (John 5:28–29)

In the resurrection of the dead, the body that is sown is perishable, but it is raised imperishable; it is sown in dishonor, but it is raised in glory; it is sown in weakness, but it is raised in power; it is sown a natural body, but it is raised a spiritual body. If there is a natural body, there is also a spiritual body. (1 Corinthians 15:42–44)

Pause to reflect on these Biblical affirmations.

Thanksgiving

We give thanks to You, Lord, and call upon Your name;
We make Your deeds known among the nations.
We sing to You, sing praises to You;
We tell of all Your wonders.
We glory in Your holy name;
Let the hearts of those who seek You, O Lord, rejoice.
   (Psalm 105:1–3)

Pause to offer your own expressions of thanksgiving.

Closing Prayer

You, O Lord, give wisdom;
From Your mouth come knowledge and understanding.

You store up sound wisdom for the upright;
You are a shield to those who walk in integrity,
Guarding the paths of the just
And protecting the way of Your saints. (Proverbs 2:6–8)

DAY 29

Adoration

How lovely are Your dwellings,
O Lord of hosts!
My soul longs and even faints for Your courts;
My heart and my flesh cry out for You, the living God.
   (Psalm 84:1–2)

Your righteousness, O God, reaches to the heavens;
You have done great things.
O God, who is like You? (Psalm 71:19)

Pause to express your thoughts of praise and worship.

Confession

Do You, O God, not see my ways
And count all my steps? (Job 31:4)

Ask the Spirit to search your heart and reveal any areas of unconfessed sin. Acknowledge these to the Lord and thank Him for His forgiveness.

Renewal

The hour has come for me to wake up from sleep, for my salvation is nearer now than when I first believed. The night is nearly over; the day is almost here. Therefore may I cast off the works of darkness and put on the armor of light. (Romans 13:11–12)

Though I walk in the flesh, I do not war according to the flesh. The weapons of my warfare are not fleshly, but divinely powerful to overthrow strongholds, casting down arguments and every pretension that sets itself up against the knowledge of You, O God, and taking every thought captive to the obedience of Christ. (2 Corinthians 10:3–5)

Pause to add your own prayers for personal renewal.

Petition

Just as I received You as Lord, Christ Jesus, so let me walk in You, rooted and built up in You, and established in the faith as I was taught, and abounding in thanksgiving. (Colossians 2:6–7)

Pause here to petition God for growth in love and compassion toward others. Offer prayers for your loved ones, for those who do not know Jesus and for those in need. Offer prayers regarding your activities for this day and any special concerns you may have.

Intercession

All things are from You, O God, who reconciled us to Yourself through Christ and gave us the ministry of reconciliation: namely, that You were reconciling the world to Yourself in Christ, not counting people's trespasses against them. And You have committed to us the message of reconciliation. Therefore we are ambassadors for Christ, as though You were appealing through us, as we implore others on Christ's behalf to be reconciled to You. (2 Corinthians 5:18–20)

Take a few moments to intercede on behalf of friends, relatives, neighbors and coworkers who do not yet know salvation in Jesus Christ.

Affirmation

You, O Lord, are the Spirit, and where Your Spirit is, there is freedom. (2 Corinthians 3:17)

You, Christ Jesus, are not weak in dealing with us, but You are powerful among us. For though You were crucified in weakness, yet You live by the power of God. Likewise, we are weak in You, yet by the power of God we will live with You to serve others. (2 Corinthians 13:3–4)

Pause to reflect on these Biblical affirmations.

Thanksgiving

I praise You, O Lord!
I will thank You with all my heart
In the council of the upright and in the assembly.
Great are Your works, O Lord;
They are pondered by all who delight in them.
Splendid and majestic is Your work,
And Your righteousness endures forever.
You have caused Your wonderful acts to be
    remembered;
You, O Lord, are gracious and compassionate.
    (Psalm 111:1–4)

Pause to offer your own expressions of thanksgiving.

Closing Prayer

To us a child is born, to us a son is given,
And the government is on Your shoulders.
And You are called Wonderful Counselor, Mighty God,
Everlasting Father, Prince of Peace.
Of the increase of Your government and peace
There will be no end.
You reign on the throne of David and over his kingdom,
Establishing and upholding it with justice and
    righteousness
From this time on and forever.
Your zeal, O Lord of hosts, will accomplish this.
    (Isaiah 9:6–7)

DAY 30

Adoration

You are my shield, my very great reward. (Genesis 15:1)

> As for You, O God, Your way is perfect;
> Your Word is proven.
> You are a shield to all who take refuge in You.
> For who is God besides You?
> And who is the Rock except You, our God?
>   (Psalm 18:30–31)

Pause to express your thoughts of praise and worship.

Confession

> Remember, O Lord, Your compassions and Your mercies,
> For they are from of old.
> Do not remember the sins of my youth or my
>   transgressions;
> According to Your loyal love remember me
> For the sake of Your goodness, O Lord. (Psalm 25:6–7)

Ask the Spirit to search your heart and reveal any areas of unconfessed sin. Acknowledge these to the Lord and thank Him for His forgiveness.

Renewal

I do not want even a hint of immorality, or any impurity or greed in my life, as these are improper for a saint. Nor will I give myself to obscenity, foolish talk or coarse joking, which are not fitting, but rather I will give myself to thanksgiving. (Ephesians 5:3–4)

Whatever is true, whatever is noble, whatever is right, whatever is pure, whatever is lovely, whatever is of good report—

if anything is excellent or praiseworthy—may I think about such things. The things I have learned and received and heard and seen in those who walk with Christ I will practice, and You, the God of peace, will be with me. (Philippians 4:8–9)

Pause to add your own prayers for personal renewal.

Petition

Answer me, O Lord, for Your lovingkindness is good;
In the abundance of Your mercies, turn to me.
(Psalm 69:16)

Pause here to petition God to help you be a faithful steward of your time, talents, possessions and relationships. Offer prayers of petition regarding your activities for this day and any special concerns you may have.

Intercession

You, the God of Israel, spoke,
You, the Rock of Israel, said to David:
"He who rules over men in righteousness,
Who rules in the fear of God,
Is like the light of morning when the sun rises,
A morning without clouds,
Or like the tender grass springing out of the earth
Through the sunshine after rain." (2 Samuel 23:3–4)

Take a few moments to intercede on behalf of your local, state or provincial, and national governments. Pray for spiritual revival in the nation and offer prayers regarding current events and concerns.

Affirmation

Those who belong to You, Christ Jesus, have crucified the flesh with its passions and desires. (Galatians 5:24)

I have put off the old self with its practices and have put on the new self, which is being renewed in full knowledge according to Your image, O my Creator. (Colossians 3:9–10)

I know that I abide in You, O Christ, and You in me, because You have given me Your Spirit. (1 John 4:13)

Pause to reflect on these Biblical affirmations.

Thanksgiving

I love You, Lord, because You heard
My voice and my supplications.
Because You turned Your ear to me,
I will call on You as long as I live. (Psalm 116:1–2)

I will give thanks to You, the God of heaven,
For Your merciful love endures forever. (Psalm 136:26)

Pause to offer your own expressions of thanksgiving.

Closing Prayer

Behold, You will come with power, Lord God,
And Your arm will rule for You.
Behold, Your reward is with You,
And Your recompense accompanies You.
You will feed Your flock like a shepherd;
You will gather the lambs in Your arms
And carry them close to Your heart;
You will gently lead those that have young.
     (Isaiah 40:10–11)

Your lovingkindness is great toward us,
And Your truth, O Lord, endures forever.
We praise You, Lord! (Psalm 117:2)

DAY 31

Adoration

Who gave You authority over the earth, O God?
Who put You in charge of the whole world?
If You set Your heart on it and withdrew Your spirit and
    Your breath,
All flesh would perish together
And people would return to dust. (Job 34:13–15)

Every animal of the forest is Yours,
And the cattle on a thousand hills.
You know every bird in the mountains,
And everything that moves in the field is Yours.
    (Psalm 50:10–11)

Pause to express your thoughts of praise and worship.

Confession

What I do may seem right to me.
But You, Lord, know what I am thinking.
    (Proverbs 21:2)

*Ask the Spirit to search your heart and reveal any areas of
unconfessed sin. Acknowledge these to the Lord and thank Him
for His forgiveness.*

Renewal

May I be holy to You, for You, the Lord, are holy, and You
have set me apart to be Your own. (Leviticus 20:26)

May I learn to fear You all the days I live on the earth and
teach Your words to my children. (Deuteronomy 4:10)

May I be careful not to forget You, O Lord my God, by failing to observe Your commandments, Your ordinances and Your statutes. (Deuteronomy 8:11)

Pause to add your own prayers for personal renewal.

Petition

I have sought You with my whole heart;
Do not let me stray from Your commands.
   (Psalm 119:10)

Pause here to offer prayers of petition regarding your family and your ministry. Ask for His help and guidance in sharing Jesus with others and helping others grow in Him. Ask for guidance in your vocation and your avocations. Offer prayers of petition regarding your activities for this day and any special concerns you may have.

Intercession

Jesus, You have called us to go and make disciples of all nations, baptizing them in the name of the Father and of the Son and of the Holy Spirit, teaching them to observe everything You have commanded us. And surely You are with us always, even to the end of the age. (Matthew 28:19–20)

Take a few moments to intercede on behalf of local, national and world missions. Pray that the Great Commission would be fulfilled and for any special concerns you may have for missions.

Affirmation

When I seek You, Lord my God, I will find You if I seek with all my heart and with all my soul. (Deuteronomy 4:29)

You are the Lord who made the earth, the Lord who formed it to establish it—the Lord is Your name and You promised this: "Call to Me, and I will answer you and tell you great and unsearchable things you do not know." (Jeremiah 33:2–3)

Your hand, O God, is favorable to everyone who looks to You, but Your power and Your anger are against all who forsake You. (Ezra 8:22)

Pause to reflect on these Biblical affirmations.

Thanksgiving

You are my God, and I will give thanks to You;
You are my God, and I will exalt You.
I will give thanks to You, Lord, for You are good;
Your loyal love endures forever. (Psalm 118:28–29)

Pause to offer your own expressions of thanksgiving.

Closing Prayer

As for me, I will always have hope,
And I will praise You more and more.
My mouth will tell of Your righteousness
And of Your salvation all day long,
Though I know not its measure.
I will come and tell of Your mighty acts;
I will proclaim Your righteousness—Yours alone.
Since my youth, O God, You have taught me,
And to this day I declare Your wondrous deeds.
     (Psalm 71:14–17)

I will lie down in peace and sleep,
For You alone, O Lord, make me dwell in safety.
     (Psalm 4:8)

THE THIRD MONTH

DAY 1

Adoration

I will bless You, Lord, at all times;
Your praise will always be in my mouth.
My soul will make its boast in You, Lord;
The humble will hear and be glad.
May all Your people magnify You with me,
And let us exalt Your name together. (Psalm 34:1–3)

You are my stronghold,
My God, You are a rock of refuge to me. (Psalm 94:22)

Pause to express your thoughts of praise and worship.

Confession

You, O Lord, have said,
"Come now, let us reason together.
Though your sins are like scarlet,
They shall be as white as snow;
Though they are red as crimson,
They shall be like wool." (Isaiah 1:18)

Ask the Spirit to search your heart and reveal any areas of unconfessed sin. Acknowledge these to the Lord and thank Him for His forgiveness.

Renewal

O Lord, may I be strong in You and in Your mighty power as I put on Your full armor, so that I will be able to stand against the schemes of the devil. (Ephesians 6:10–11)

Since I belong to the day, may I be self-controlled, putting on faith and love as a breastplate, and the hope of salvation as a helmet. (1 Thessalonians 5:8)

Pause to add your own prayers for personal renewal.

Petition

O Lord, I cry to You; hasten to me.
Hear my voice when I cry to You.
Let my prayer be set before You like incense,
And the lifting up of my hands like the evening
    sacrifice. (Psalm 141:1–2)

Pause here to petition God for growth in your character and personal discipline, and for physical health and strength. Ask that He empower you for spiritual warfare against the temptations of the world, the flesh and the devil. Offer prayers regarding your activities for this day and any special concerns you may have.

Intercession

Restore us again, O God of our salvation,
And put away Your anger toward us.
Will You be angry with us forever?
Will You prolong Your anger to all generations?
Will You not revive us again,
That Your people may rejoice in You?
Show us Your lovingkindness, O Lord,
And grant us Your salvation. (Psalm 85:4–7)

Take a few moments to intercede on behalf of the poor and hungry, the oppressed and persecuted, and those in control of world and national resources. Offer prayers for peace among nations and regarding current events and concerns.

Affirmation

You Yourself go before me and will be with me, Lord; You
will never leave me nor forsake me. I will not be afraid or be
dismayed. (Deuteronomy 31:8)

> You, O Lord, will guard the feet of Your saints,
> But the wicked will be silenced in darkness.
> It is not by strength that one prevails;
> Those who contend with You will be shattered.
> You will thunder against them from heaven;
> You will judge the ends of the earth.
> You will give strength to Your king
> And exalt the horn of Your anointed. (1 Samuel 2:9–10)

Pause to reflect on these Biblical affirmations.

Thanksgiving

In the day that You created Your people, You made them in
Your likeness. You created them male and female and blessed
them in the day they were created. (Genesis 5:1–2)

> It was You, Lord,
> Who created the heavens and stretched them out,
> Who spread out the earth and all that grows on it;
> You give breath to its people,
> And spirit to those who walk on it. (Isaiah 42:5)

Pause to offer your own expressions of thanksgiving.

Closing Prayer

> I rejoice at Your word
> As one who finds great spoil.
> I hate and abhor falsehood,
> But I love Your law.

Great peace have they who love Your law,
And nothing causes them to stumble.
O Lord, I hope for Your salvation,
And I follow Your commands.
My soul keeps Your testimonies,
For I love them greatly.
I keep Your precepts and Your testimonies,
For all my ways are known to You.
    (Psalm 119:162–163, 165–168)

DAY 2

Adoration

Like the roar of rushing waters and like loud peals of thunder, a great multitude will shout, "Hallelujah! For You reign, Lord God Almighty. Let us rejoice and be glad and give You glory! For the marriage of the Lamb has come, and His bride has made herself ready." Blessed are those who are invited to the marriage supper of the Lamb. (Revelation 19:6–7, 9)

Lord Jesus, You are the Root and the Offspring of David, the bright Morning Star. (Revelation 22:16)

Pause to express your thoughts of praise and worship.

Confession

> We will return to You, O Lord.
> For You have torn us, but You will heal us;
> You have injured us, but You will bind up our wounds.
> After two days You will revive us;
> On the third day You will raise us up,
> That we may live before You. (Hosea 6:1–2)

Ask the Spirit to search your heart and reveal any areas of unconfessed sin. Acknowledge these to the Lord and thank Him for His forgiveness.

Renewal

O God, may I rejoice always, pray without ceasing, and give thanks in all circumstances, for this is Your will for me in Christ Jesus. (1 Thessalonians 5:16–18)

I want to know You, O Christ, and the power of Your resurrection and the fellowship of Your sufferings, being conformed to Your death, that I may attain to the resurrection from the dead. (Philippians 3:10–11)

Pause to add your own prayers for personal renewal.

Petition

> Hear my cry, O God,
> And listen to my prayer.
> From the ends of the earth I call to You
> When my heart grows faint;
> Lead me to the rock that is higher than I.
> You have been a shelter for me
> And a strong tower against the enemy.
> I will dwell in Your tent forever
> And take refuge in the shelter of Your wings.
>   (Psalm 61:1–4)

Pause here to petition God for growth in your desire to know and please Jesus Christ. Pray for a greater love and commitment to Him, for the grace to practice His presence and for the grace to glorify Him in your life. Offer prayers regarding your activities for this day and any special concerns you may have.

Intercession

Triune God, we rejoice in the unity we have in You, in which there is one body and one Spirit, just as we were called in one hope of our calling; one Lord, one faith, one baptism, one God and Father of all, who is over all and through all and in all. (Ephesians 4:4–6)

Take a few moments to intercede on behalf of your local church, other churches, evangelism and discipleship ministries, educational ministries and any other special concerns you may have.

Affirmation

You who are the Glory of Israel do not lie or change Your mind, for You are not a man, that You should change Your mind. (1 Samuel 15:29)

> Your counsel stands firm forever, O Lord,
> The plans of Your heart through all generations.
>   (Psalm 33:11)

O Lord, You are not slow concerning Your promise, as some count slowness, but You are patient with us, not wanting anyone to perish but all to come to repentance. (2 Peter 3:9)

Pause to reflect on these Biblical affirmations.

Thanksgiving

You, O Lord, are a merciful God; You will not forsake us or destroy us or forget the covenant with our forefathers, which You swore to them. (Deuteronomy 4:31)

> You, O Lord, are a shield around me;
> You bestow glory on me and lift up my head.
>   (Psalm 3:3)

Pause to offer your own expressions of thanksgiving.

Closing Prayer

By this Your love was manifested to us: that You sent Your only begotten Son into the world that we might live through Him. This is love: not that we loved You, but that You loved us and sent Your Son to be the propitiation for our sins. (1 John 4:9–10)

Lord, the love we have from You is patient, it is kind, it does not envy; love does not boast, it is not arrogant, it does not behave rudely; it does not seek its own, it is not provoked, it keeps no record of wrongs; it does not rejoice in unright-eousness but rejoices with the truth; it bears all things, believes all things, hopes all things, endures all things. Love never fails. (1 Corinthians 13:4–8)

DAY 3

Adoration

I will praise You with uprightness of heart
As I learn Your righteous judgments. (Psalm 119:7)

Lord, I know that You are great,
And that You are above all gods.
You do what pleases You,
In the heavens and on the earth,
In the seas and all their depths. (Psalm 135:5–6)

Pause to express your thoughts of praise and worship.

Confession

If I say that I have fellowship with You, O Christ, and yet
walk in the darkness, I lie and do not practice the truth. But
if I walk in the light, as You are in the light, I have fellowship with others, and Your blood, O Jesus, purifies me from
all sin. (1 John 1:6–7)

*Ask the Spirit to search your heart and reveal any areas of
unconfessed sin. Acknowledge these to the Lord and thank Him
for His forgiveness.*

Renewal

May I be a doer of the word and not merely a hearer who
deceives myself. For if I am a hearer of the word and not a
doer, I am like those who look at their natural faces in a mirror, and after looking at themselves, go away, and immedi-
ately forget what kind of people they were. But if I look
intently into the perfect law of freedom and continue in it
and I am not a forgetful hearer but a doer of the word, I will
be blessed in what I do. (James 1:22–25)

In obedience to the truth, may I purify my soul for a sincere love of my brothers and sisters, and love others fervently from my heart. (1 Peter 1:22)

Pause to add your own prayers for personal renewal.

Petition

May I not say when I am tempted, "I am being tempted by God"; for You, O God, cannot be tempted by evil, nor do You tempt anyone. But each one of us is tempted when we are drawn away and enticed by our own lust. Then, after lust has conceived, it gives birth to sin; and sin, when it is full-grown, gives birth to death. (James 1:13–15)

Pause here to petition God for wisdom. Ask Him to develop your eternal perspective, to renew your mind with truth and to help you develop greater skill in each area of your life. Offer prayers regarding your activities for this day and any special concerns you may have.

Intercession

Far be it from me that I should sin against You, O Lord, by ceasing to pray for others. (1 Samuel 12:23)

Take a few moments to intercede on behalf of your immediate family and other relatives. Offer prayers for their spiritual, emotional and physical concerns.

Affirmation

It is for my good that You, Jesus, returned to the Father, because You have sent the Counselor, the Holy Spirit, to me. (John 16:7)

Jesus, You told Your disciples, "The Spirit will glorify Me by taking from what is Mine and making it known to you. All that belongs to the Father is Mine. That is why I said that He will take from what is Mine and make it known to you." (John 16:14–15)

Pause to reflect on these Biblical affirmations.

Thanksgiving

I trust in Your loyal love;
My heart rejoices in Your salvation.
I will sing to You, O Lord,
For You have dealt bountifully with me. (Psalm 13:5–6)

I bless You, Lord,
For You have heard the voice of my prayers.
You are my strength and my shield;
My heart trusts in You, and I am helped.
My heart greatly rejoices,
And I will give thanks to You in song. (Psalm 28:6–7)

Pause to offer your own expressions of thanksgiving.

Closing Prayer

You are worthy, our Lord and God,
To receive glory and honor and power,
For You created all things,
And by Your will they were created and have their
    being. (Revelation 4:11)

Every creature in heaven and on earth and under the earth and on the sea and all that is in them will sing to You:

"To Him who sits on the throne and to the Lamb
Be blessing and honor and glory and power
For ever and ever!" (Revelation 5:13)

DAY 4

Adoration

You, O Lord, are the One who stretches out the heavens, lays the foundation of the earth, and forms the spirits of all people within them. (Zechariah 12:1)

You are the Lord, the God who created the spirits of all people. (Numbers 27:16)

Nothing is too difficult for You, Lord. (Genesis 18:14)

Pause to express your thoughts of praise and worship.

Confession

> Death and Destruction lie open before You, O Lord;
> How much more do human hearts! (Proverbs 15:11)

Ask the Spirit to search your heart and reveal any areas of unconfessed sin. Acknowledge these to the Lord and thank Him for His forgiveness.

Renewal

May I observe all Your statutes and all Your judgments and follow them; You are the Lord. (Leviticus 19:37)

May I not show partiality in judgment, but hear both small and great alike. May I not be afraid of anyone, for judgment belongs to You, O God. (Deuteronomy 1:17)

Pause to add your own prayers for personal renewal.

Petition

> No one who waits for You will be ashamed,
> But those who are treacherous without cause will be
>   ashamed.

Show me Your ways, O Lord,
Teach me Your paths;
Lead me in Your truth and teach me,
For You are the God of my salvation,
And my hope is in You all day long. (Psalm 25:3–5)

Pause here to petition God for spiritual insight so that you might have understanding of His Word. Ask for insight into your identity in Jesus Christ: that you might know who you are, what direction your life should take and what His purpose for your life is. Offer prayers regarding your activities for this day and any special concerns you may have.

Intercession

We want to serve You, O God, in every way: in great endurance, in afflictions, in needs, in distresses, in beatings, in imprisonments, in tumults, in labors, in sleeplessness, in hunger, in purity, in knowledge, in patience, in kindness, in the Holy Spirit, in sincere love, in the word of truth, in Your power, O God—through the weapons of righteousness in the right hand and in the left, through glory and dishonor, through bad report and good report—as deceivers, and yet true; as unknown, and yet well-known; as dying, and yet living; as beaten, and yet not killed; as sorrowful, yet always rejoicing; as poor, yet making many rich; as having nothing, and yet possessing everything. (2 Corinthians 6:4–10)

Take a few moments to intercede on behalf of other believers, such as your personal friends, those in ministry and those who are oppressed and in need.

Affirmation

O Lord, what are human beings that You take care of them,
Or people that You think of them?

They are like breaths;
Their days are like passing shadows. (Psalm 144:3–4)

Those who seek to keep their life will lose it, and those who lose their life will preserve it. (Luke 17:33)

Here I do not have an enduring city, but I am seeking the city that is to come. (Hebrews 13:14)

Pause to reflect on these Biblical affirmations.

Thanksgiving

I will declare Your name to my brothers and sisters;
In the midst of the congregation I will praise You.
All who fear You, praise You, O Lord!
All the descendants of Jacob glorify You!
All the descendants of Israel stand in awe of You!
For You have not despised or disdained the suffering of
    the afflicted one;
You have not hidden Your face from him,
But You have listened to his cry for help.
    (Psalm 22:22–24)

Pause to offer your own expressions of thanksgiving.

Closing Prayer

O Lord, You will be gracious to whom You will be gracious, and You will have compassion on whom You will have compassion. (Exodus 33:19)

You, Lord God, are compassionate and gracious, slow to anger, and abounding in lovingkindness and truth, maintaining love to thousands, and forgiving iniquity, transgression and sin. (Exodus 34:6–7)

DAY 5

Adoration

Where does wisdom come from?
Where does understanding dwell?
It is hidden from the eyes of every living thing
And concealed from the birds of the air.
Destruction and Death say,
"Only a rumor of it has reached our ears."
You understand its way, O God,
And You know its place.
For You look to the ends of the earth
And see everything under the heavens. (Job 28:20–24)

We fear You, O God,
Because You care about those who are wise. (Job 37:24)

Pause to express your thoughts of praise and worship.

Confession

O God, You know my foolishness,
And my guilt is not hidden from You.
May those who hope in You not be ashamed because of
    me, O Lord God of hosts;
May those who seek You not be dishonored because of
    me, O God of Israel. (Psalm 69:5–6)

*Ask the Spirit to search your heart and reveal any areas of
unconfessed sin. Acknowledge these to the Lord and thank Him
for His forgiveness.*

Renewal

Solomon asked You, O Lord, "Give me wisdom and knowledge, that I may lead this people, for who is able to judge

this great people of Yours?" You answered Solomon saying, "Because this was in your heart and you have not asked for riches, wealth or honor, nor for the life of your enemies, and since you have not asked for a long life but for wisdom and knowledge to judge My people over whom I have made you king, wisdom and knowledge will be given you. And I will also give you riches and wealth and honor, such as no king who was before you ever had and none after you will have." (2 Chronicles 1:10–12)

May I not be worried and troubled about many things; only one thing is needed. Like Mary, may I choose what is better, which will not be taken away from me. (Luke 10:41–42)

Pause to add your own prayers for personal renewal.

Petition

May everything I do be done in love. (1 Corinthians 16:14)

Pause here to petition God for growth in love and compassion toward others. Offer prayers for your loved ones, for those who do not know Jesus and for those in need. Offer prayers regarding your activities for this day and any special concerns you may have.

Intercession

I pray that words may be given to me, that I may open my mouth boldly to make known the mystery of the gospel. (Ephesians 6:19)

Take a few moments to intercede on behalf of friends, relatives, neighbors and coworkers who do not yet know salvation in Jesus Christ.

Affirmation

The mouths of the righteous speak wisdom,
And their tongues speak what is just.

Your law is in their hearts, O God;
Their steps do not slide. (Psalm 37:30–31)

We should be quick to hear, slow to speak and slow to anger,
for our anger does not produce Your righteousness, O God.
(James 1:19–20)

Pause to reflect on these Biblical affirmations.

Thanksgiving

The heavens declare Your glory, O God,
And the skies proclaim the work of Your hands.
Day after day they pour forth speech;
Night after night they reveal knowledge. (Psalm 19:1–2)

I will exalt You, O Lord, for You lifted me up
And did not let my enemies rejoice over me.
O Lord my God,
I cried to You for help and You healed me. (Psalm 30:1–2)

Pause to offer your own expressions of thanksgiving.

Closing Prayer

As for You, O God, Your way is perfect;
Your word, O Lord, is proven.
You are a shield for all who take refuge in You.
For who are You besides the Lord?
And who is the Rock except You, our God?
    (2 Samuel 22:31–32)

DAY 6

Adoration

You have chosen me as Your witness and servant so that I may know and believe You and understand that You are the Lord. Before You no god was formed nor will there be one after You. (Isaiah 43:10)

> You are the Lord, Israel's King
> And Redeemer, the Lord of hosts;
> You have said, "I am the first and I am the last;
> Apart from Me there is no God." (Isaiah 44:6)

Pause to express your thoughts of praise and worship.

Confession

> Can human beings be more righteous than You, O God?
> Can we be more pure than our Maker? (Job 4:17)

Ask the Spirit to search your heart and reveal any areas of unconfessed sin. Acknowledge these to the Lord and thank Him for His forgiveness.

Renewal

When I have done all the things You have commanded me, let me realize that I am an unworthy servant; I have only done what I ought to have done. (Luke 17:10)

May I do Your work, O God, while it is day; night is coming, when no one can work. (John 9:4)

Pause to add your own prayers for personal renewal.

Petition

May I be a person who fears You, O God, who loves truth and who hates dishonest gain. (Exodus 18:21)

Pause here to petition God to help you be a faithful steward of your time, talents, possessions and relationships. Offer prayers of petition regarding your activities for this day and any special concerns you may have.

Intercession

Righteousness exalts a nation,
But sin is a disgrace to any people. (Proverbs 14:34)

Take a few moments to intercede on behalf of your local, state or provincial, and national governments. Pray for spiritual revival in the nation and offer prayers regarding current events and concerns.

Affirmation

Lord, teach me humility:

You save the humble
But bring low those whose eyes are haughty. (Psalm 18:27)

Pride breeds nothing but strife,
But wisdom is found in those who take advice.
   (Proverbs 13:10)

When pride comes, then comes dishonor,
But with humility comes wisdom. (Proverbs 11:2)

The proud will be humbled
And the lofty brought low;
You alone, O Lord, will be exalted. (Isaiah 2:11)

Pause to reflect on these Biblical affirmations.

Thanksgiving

How great is Your goodness,
Which You have stored up for those who fear You,
Which You have prepared for those who take refuge in
    You
In the sight of others! (Psalm 31:19)

Surely You are my helper, O God;
You are the sustainer of my soul. (Psalm 54:4)

Pause to offer your own expressions of thanksgiving.

Closing Prayer

God, You are my strong fortress
And You make my way perfect.
You make my feet like the feet of a deer;
You enable me to stand on the heights.
You train my hands for battle
So that my arms can bend a bow of bronze.
You give me Your shield of salvation;
You stoop down to make me great.
You broaden the path beneath me,
And my feet have not slipped. (2 Samuel 22:33–37;
    Psalm 18:33–36)

You live, O Lord. I bless You, my Rock!
May You be exalted, O Rock of my salvation!
    (2 Samuel 22:47; Psalm 18:46)

DAY 7

Adoration

We see you, Jesus—the One who was made a little lower than the angels—now crowned with glory and honor because You suffered death, so that by the grace of God You might taste death for everyone. In bringing many of us to glory, it was fitting that God, for whom and through whom everything exists, should make You—the author of our salvation—perfect through suffering. (Hebrews 2:9–10)

You are the King of kings and Lord of lords. (Revelation 19:16)

Pause to express your thoughts of praise and worship.

Confession

We know in our hearts that parents discipline their children; so You, the Lord our God, discipline us. (Deuteronomy 8:5)

Ask the Spirit to search your heart and reveal any areas of unconfessed sin. Acknowledge these to the Lord and thank Him for His forgiveness.

Renewal

May I not receive Your grace, O God, in vain. For You have said, "In the acceptable time I heard you, and in the day of salvation I helped you." Now is the time of Your favor; now is the day of salvation. (2 Corinthians 6:1–2)

Lord, may You establish my heart as blameless and holy in Your presence at the coming of our Lord Jesus with all His saints. (1 Thessalonians 3:13)

Pause to add your own prayers for personal renewal.

Petition

May I obey those who are in authority over me in all things, not with external service as one who pleases people, but with sincerity of heart, fearing You, Lord. Whatever I do, may I work at it with all my heart, as working for You and not for people, knowing that I will receive the reward of the inheritance from You. It is the Lord Christ I am serving. (Colossians 3:22–24)

Pause here to offer prayers of petition regarding your family and your ministry. Ask for His help and guidance in sharing Jesus with others and helping others grow in Him. Ask for guidance in your vocation and your avocations. Offer prayers of petition regarding your activities for this day and any special concerns you may have.

Intercession

O God, in the past You overlooked the times of ignorance, but now You command all people everywhere to repent. For You have set a day when You will judge the world with justice by the Man You have appointed. You have given assurance of this to all people by raising Him from the dead. (Acts 17:30–31)

Take a few moments to intercede on behalf of local, national and world missions. Pray that the Great Commission would be fulfilled and for any special concerns you may have for missions.

Affirmation

Only in You, O Lord, are righteousness and strength. (Isaiah 45:24)

O God, You who made the world and everything in it are Lord of heaven and earth, and You do not dwell in temples built by hands. You are not served by human hands, as though You needed anything, because You Yourself give all people life and breath and everything else. (Acts 17:24–25)

Pause to reflect on these Biblical affirmations.

Thanksgiving

I will sing of Your strength,
Yes, I will sing of Your mercy in the morning,
For You have been my stronghold,
My refuge in times of trouble.
To You, O my strength, I will sing praises,
For You are my fortress, my loving God.
  (Psalm 59:16–17)

Pause to offer your own expressions of thanksgiving.

Closing Prayer

I would have lost heart unless I had believed
That I would see Your goodness, O Lord,
In the land of the living.
I will hope in You and be of good courage,
And You will strengthen my heart;
Yes, I will hope in You, O Lord. (Psalm 27:13–14)

My soul waits in hope for You, O Lord;
You are my help and my shield.
My heart rejoices in You,
Because I trust in Your holy name.
Let Your unfailing love be upon me, O Lord,
Even as I put my hope in You. (Psalm 33:20–22)

DAY 8

Adoration

> You, O Lord of hosts, will be exalted in judgment,
> And You, holy God, will show Yourself holy in
>   righteousness. (Isaiah 5:16)

> You long to be gracious and rise to show compassion.
> For You are a God of justice;
> Blessed are all those who wait for You! (Isaiah 30:18)

Pause to express your thoughts of praise and worship.

Confession

> Lord, there are six things You hate,
> Seven that are detestable to You:
> Haughty eyes, a lying tongue,
> Hands that shed innocent blood,
> A heart that devises wicked plans,
> Feet that run swiftly to evil,
> A false witness who breathes lies,
> And one who causes strife among brothers and sisters.
>   (Proverbs 6:16–19)

Ask the Spirit to search your heart and reveal any areas of unconfessed sin. Acknowledge these to the Lord and thank Him for His forgiveness.

Renewal

I greatly rejoice in my salvation, even though now, for a little while, I grieve because of various trials. They come so that my faith, though much more precious than gold that perishes, even though it is refined by fire, may be proved genuine and that it may result in praise, glory and honor when You are revealed, O Jesus Christ. (1 Peter 1:6–7)

Since Your day, O Lord, will come like a thief, what kind of person should I be? In holy conduct and godliness I am to look forward to Your coming day. According to Your promise, I am looking for a new heaven and a new earth where righteousness will dwell. Therefore, since I am looking for these things, may I be diligent to be found at peace with You, pure and blameless before You. (2 Peter 3:10–14)

Pause to add your own prayers for personal renewal.

Petition

The people of this world are more shrewd in dealing with their own kind than are the people of light. May I use worldly wealth to help others, making friends for myself, so that when it is gone, they may welcome me into Your eternal dwellings. (Luke 16:8–9)

Pause here to petition God for growth in your character and personal discipline, and for physical health and strength. Ask that He empower you for spiritual warfare against the temptations of the world, the flesh and the devil. Offer prayers regarding your activities for this day and any special concerns you may have.

Intercession

The end of all things is near; therefore, I should be clear minded and self-controlled so that I can pray. (1 Peter 4:7)

Take a few moments to intercede on behalf of the poor and hungry, the oppressed and persecuted, and those in control of world and national resources. Offer prayers for peace among nations and regarding current events and concerns.

Affirmation

> Your eyes are too pure to look at evil;
> You cannot look on wickedness. (Habakkuk 1:13)

Far be it from You to kill the righteous along with the wicked, treating the righteous and the wicked alike. Far be it from You! Won't You, the Judge of all the earth, do right? (Genesis 18:25)

By Your word, O God, the heavens existed long ago and the earth was formed out of water and by water. By water also the world of that time was deluged and destroyed. And by Your word the present heavens and earth are reserved for fire, being kept for the day of judgment and the destruction of ungodly men. (2 Peter 3:5–7)

Pause to reflect on these Biblical affirmations.

Thanksgiving

> I am continually with You;
> You hold me by my right hand.
> You guide me with Your counsel,
> And afterward You will take me to glory.
>   (Psalm 73:23–24)

Pause to offer your own expressions of thanksgiving.

Closing Prayer

> I will be still and know that You are God;
> You will be exalted among the nations;
> You will be exalted in the earth. (Psalm 46:10)

> I bless You, O Lord, the God of Israel,
> From everlasting to everlasting.
> Amen and Amen. (Psalm 41:13)

DAY 9

Adoration

Lord, You are a consuming fire, a jealous God. (Deuteronomy 4:24)

You are seated on Your throne with all the host of heaven standing by You on Your right and on Your left. (1 Kings 22:19)

The heavens, even the highest heavens, cannot contain You, O Lord. (2 Chronicles 2:6; 6:18)

Pause to express your thoughts of praise and worship.

Confession

> This is what You, the Lord God, the Holy One of Israel, have said:

"In repentance and rest is your salvation;
In quietness and trust is your strength." (Isaiah 30:15)

Ask the Spirit to search your heart and reveal any areas of unconfessed sin. Acknowledge these to the Lord and thank Him for His forgiveness.

Renewal

May I do what is good and right in Your sight, O Lord my God. (2 Chronicles 14:2)

May my heart take delight in Your ways, O Lord, and may I remove the places of idolatry from my life. (2 Chronicles 17:6)

Pause to add your own prayers for personal renewal.

Petition

> May I put away perversity from my mouth
> And keep corrupt talk far from my lips. (Proverbs 4:24)

Pause here to petition God for growth in your desire to know and please Jesus Christ. Pray for a greater love and commitment to Him, for the grace to practice His presence and for the grace to glorify Him in your life. Offer prayers regarding your activities for this day and any special concerns you may have.

Intercession

As living stones, we are being built into a spiritual house to be a holy priesthood, offering spiritual sacrifices acceptable to You, O God, through Jesus Christ. We are a chosen people, a royal priesthood, a holy nation, a people for Your own possession, that we may declare Your praises—You who called us out of darkness into Your marvelous light. (1 Peter 2:5, 9)

Take a few moments to intercede on behalf of your local church, other churches, evangelism and discipleship ministries, educational ministries and any other special concerns you may have.

Affirmation

How shall we escape if we ignore Your great salvation, O God? This salvation, which was first announced by the Lord Jesus, was confirmed by those who heard Him. You also bore witness to it by signs, wonders and various miracles, and gifts of Your Holy Spirit distributed according to Your will. (Hebrews 2:3–4)

The faith of Your chosen people, and the knowledge of the truth that leads to godliness, is faith and knowledge resting in the hope of eternal life. It is an eternal life that You promised before the beginning of time—and You do not lie. At the appointed time, You manifested Your word through

the preaching entrusted to the apostles by Your command,
O God our Savior. (Titus 1:1–3)

Pause to reflect on these Biblical affirmations.

Thanksgiving

I will give thanks to You, O Lord, for You are good;
Your lovingkindness endures forever. (Psalm 118:1)

Your word is settled in heaven forever, O Lord.
Your faithfulness continues through all generations;
You established the earth, and it stands.
Your laws continue to this day according to Your
    purposes,
For all things serve You. (Psalm 119:89–91)

Pause to offer your own expressions of thanksgiving.

Closing Prayer

My soul silently waits for You alone, O God;
My salvation comes from You.
You alone are my rock and my salvation;
You are my stronghold; I will never be shaken.
    (Psalm 62:1–2)

May You be blessed, O Lord God of Israel,
From everlasting to everlasting.
I praise You, O Lord. (Psalm 106:48)

DAY 10

Adoration

My soul will rejoice in You, Lord,
And delight in Your salvation. (Psalm 35:9)

O God, You are my God;
Earnestly I seek You;
My soul thirsts for You,
My body longs for You,
In a dry and weary land
Where there is no water. (Psalm 63:1)

Pause to express your thoughts of praise and worship.

Confession

Who is a God like You, who pardons iniquity
And forgives the transgression of the remnant of Your
    inheritance?
You do not stay angry forever
But delight to show mercy.
You will have compassion on Your people;
You will tread their iniquities underfoot
And hurl all their sins into the depths of the sea.
    (Micah 7:18–19)

*Ask the Spirit to search your heart and reveal any areas of
unconfessed sin. Acknowledge these to the Lord and thank Him
for His forgiveness.*

Renewal

May I be on my guard against all covetousness, for my life
does not consist in the abundance of my possessions. (Luke
12:15)

May I keep my life free from the love of money and be content with what I have, for You have said, "I will never leave you, nor will I forsake you." (Hebrews 13:5)

Pause to add your own prayers for personal renewal.

Petition

My eyes are upon You, O Sovereign Lord;
In You I take refuge; You will not leave my soul
    destitute. (Psalm 141:8)

Pause here to petition God for wisdom. Ask Him to develop your eternal perspective, to renew your mind with truth and to help you develop greater skill in each area of your life. Offer prayers regarding your activities for this day and any special concerns you may have.

Intercession

Out of the riches of Your glory, Father, strengthen Your children with power through Your Spirit in their inner being, so that Christ may dwell in their hearts through faith. And may they, being rooted and grounded in love, be able to comprehend with all the saints the width and length and height and depth of the love of Christ. And may they know this love that surpasses knowledge, that they may be filled to the measure of all Your fullness. (Ephesians 3:16–19)

Take a few moments to intercede on behalf of your immediate family and other relatives. Offer prayers for their spiritual, emotional and physical concerns.

Affirmation

Faith is the certainty of things hoped for and the conviction of things not seen. (Hebrews 11:1)

Without faith it is impossible to please You, O God, for the one who comes to You must believe that You exist, and that You are a rewarder of those who earnestly seek You. (Hebrews 11:6)

Pause to reflect on these Biblical affirmations.

Thanksgiving

Even to my old age, You are the same,
And even when my hair is gray, You will carry me.
You have made me, and You will bear me;
You will sustain me, and You will deliver me.
   (Isaiah 46:4)

I will watch in hope for You, O Lord;
I will wait for You, the God of my salvation;
You will hear me. (Micah 7:7)

Pause to offer your own expressions of thanksgiving.

Closing Prayer

Ah, Lord God! You have made the heavens and the earth by Your great power and outstretched arm. Nothing is too difficult for You. You are the great and mighty God, whose name is the Lord of hosts. You are great in counsel and mighty in deed, and Your eyes see everything that people do. You reward each of us according to our ways and according to the fruit of our deeds. (Jeremiah 32:17–19)

I delight to do Your will, O my God,
And Your law is within my heart. (Psalm 40:8)

DAY 11

Adoration

All the earth sings joyfully to You, O God!
The earth sings the glory of Your name,
Making Your praise glorious.
We say to You, "How awesome are Your works!
Through the greatness of Your power
Your enemies submit themselves to You.
All the earth will worship You
And sing praises to You;
They will sing praise to Your name." (Psalm 66:1–4)

My mouth is filled with Your praise,
And with Your glory all day long. (Psalm 71:8)

Pause to express your thoughts of praise and worship.

Confession

Before my downfall, my heart is haughty,
But I must have humility before I have honor.
    (Proverbs 18:12)

*Ask the Spirit to search your heart and reveal any areas of
unconfessed sin. Acknowledge these to the Lord and thank Him
for His forgiveness.*

Renewal

May I not turn my heart away from You, O God of Israel,
but do what You have commanded. (1 Kings 11:9–10)

May I do what is good and right and true before You, O
Lord my God, by seeking You with all my heart. (2 Chronicles 31:20–21)

Pause to add your own prayers for personal renewal.

Petition

Preserve me, O God, for I take refuge in You.
I say to You, "You are my Lord;
I have no goodness apart from You." (Psalm 16:1–2)

Pause here to petition God for spiritual insight so that you might have understanding of His Word. Ask for insight into your identity in Jesus Christ: that you might know who you are, what direction your life should take and what His purpose for your life is. Offer prayers regarding your activities for this day and any special concerns you may have.

Intercession

Lord Jesus Christ, grant that as Your body, we might reach unity in the faith and knowledge of You, the Son of God, so that we will become mature and attain to the whole measure of Your fullness. Then we will no longer be infants, being blown and carried by every wind of doctrine and by the cunning and craftiness of people who scheme deceitfully. Instead, we will speak the truth in love; we will grow up in every way in You, our Head. (Ephesians 4:13–15)

Take a few moments to intercede on behalf of other believers, such as your personal friends, those in ministry and those who are oppressed and in need.

Affirmation

I have come to Mount Zion, to the heavenly Jerusalem, Your city, O living God, to myriads of angels, and to the assembly and church of the firstborn who are enrolled in heaven. I have come to You, the Judge of all, to the spirits of the righteous made perfect, to Jesus the mediator of a new covenant, and to the sprinkled blood that speaks better things than the blood of Abel. (Hebrews 12:22–24)

Those who overcome will be clothed in white garments, and
You, Jesus, will not blot out their names from the book of
life, but You will confess their names before Your Father and
before His angels. (Revelation 3:5)

Pause to reflect on these Biblical affirmations.

Thanksgiving

O God, our Father, You presented Christ as a sacrifice of
atonement through faith in His blood. You did this to
demonstrate Your righteousness, because in Your mercy You
passed over the sins committed before Jesus died. You did it
to demonstrate Your righteousness in the present time, that
You might be just and the justifier of those who have faith
in Jesus. (Romans 3:25–26)

Having been justified by faith, I have peace with You, O
God, through the Lord Jesus Christ, through whom I have
gained access by faith into this grace in which I stand; and I
rejoice in the hope of Your glory. (Romans 5:1–2)

Pause to offer your own expressions of thanksgiving.

Closing Prayer

   Your word is a lamp to my feet
   And a light to my path.
   I have inclined my heart to perform Your statutes
   To the very end. (Psalm 119:105, 112)

DAY 12

Adoration

> I will exalt You and worship You,
> For You, Lord God, are holy. (Psalm 99:9)

> I have tasted and seen that You, O Lord, are good;
> Blessed is the one who takes refuge in You!
> All Your saints fear You,
> For those who fear You lack nothing. (Psalm 34:8–9)

Pause to express your thoughts of praise and worship.

Confession

May we not sin against You, Father. But if anyone sins, we have an Advocate with You; He is Jesus Christ, the Righteous. And He is the propitiation for our sins, and not for ours only but also for the whole world. (1 John 2:1–2)

Ask the Spirit to search your heart and reveal any areas of unconfessed sin. Acknowledge these to the Lord and thank Him for His forgiveness.

Renewal

May I not let my heart be troubled; let me trust in You, O God, and trust also in Christ. (John 14:1)

Jesus, as the Father has loved You, You also have loved me. May I abide in Your love. If I keep Your commandments, I will abide in Your love, just as You kept Your Father's commandments and abide in His love. You have told me this so that Your joy may be in me and that my joy may be full. (John 15:9–11)

May I never boast except in Your cross, Lord Jesus Christ, through which the world has been crucified to me, and I to the world. (Galatians 6:14)

Pause to add your own prayers for personal renewal.

Petition

May I walk in wisdom toward outsiders, making the most of every opportunity. My speech should always be graceful, seasoned with salt, so that I may know how to answer each person. (Colossians 4:5–6)

Pause here to petition God for growth in love and compassion toward others. Offer prayers for your loved ones, for those who do not know Jesus and for those in need. Offer prayers regarding your activities for this day and any special concerns you may have.

Intercession

O God, open to me a door for the word, so that I may speak the mystery of Christ and proclaim it clearly, as I ought. (Colossians 4:3–4)

Take a few moments to intercede on behalf of friends, relatives, neighbors and coworkers who do not yet know salvation in Jesus Christ.

Affirmation

Blessed are those who make You their trust, O Lord,
Who do not look to the proud or those who turn aside
    to lies. (Psalm 40:4)

I will call upon You and come and pray to You, and You will listen to me. I will seek You and find You when I search for You with all my heart. (Jeremiah 29:12–13)

Pause to reflect on these Biblical affirmations.

Thanksgiving

Lord Jesus Christ, if I have been united with You in the likeness of Your death, I will certainly also be united with You in the likeness of Your resurrection. (Romans 6:5)

I thank You, God, because of Your grace in Christ Jesus. In Him we have been enriched in every way, in all speech and in all knowledge. We do not lack any spiritual gift, as we eagerly wait for the revelation of our Lord Jesus Christ. (1 Corinthians 1:4–5, 7)

Pause to offer your own expressions of thanksgiving.

Closing Prayer

Lord Jesus, You are the stone that was rejected by the builders, but that has become the chief cornerstone. Salvation is found in no one else, for there is no other name under heaven given to us by which we can be saved. (Acts 4:11–12)

I believe that You, Jesus, are the Christ, the Son of God, and by believing, I have life in Your name. (John 20:31)

DAY 13

Adoration

You, O Lord, execute righteousness
And justice for all who are oppressed.
You are compassionate and gracious,
Slow to anger and abounding in lovingkindness.
　(Psalm 103:6, 8)

Righteousness and justice are the foundation of Your
　throne;
Lovingkindness and truth go before You. (Psalm 89:14)

Pause to express your thoughts of praise and worship.

Confession

What can I say to You? What can I speak? How can I justify
myself? You have uncovered the iniquity of Your servant.
(Genesis 44:16)

*Ask the Spirit to search your heart and reveal any areas of
unconfessed sin. Acknowledge these to the Lord and thank Him
for His forgiveness.*

Renewal

May I walk properly as in the daytime, not in partying and
drunkenness, not in sexual immorality and evil conduct, not
in dissension and jealousy. Rather, may I put on You like
clothing, Lord Jesus Christ, rather than thinking about how
to satisfy my fleshly lusts. (Romans 13:13–14)

Since I have Your promises, O God, may I cleanse myself
from all pollution of body and spirit, perfecting holiness in
the fear of You. (2 Corinthians 7:1)

Pause to add your own prayers for personal renewal.

Petition

We are all children of the light and children of the day. We do not belong to the night or to the darkness. So then, let us not be like others who are asleep, but let us be alert and self-controlled. (1 Thessalonians 5:5–6)

Pause here to petition God to help you be a faithful steward of your time, talents, possessions and relationships. Offer prayers of petition regarding your activities for this day and any special concerns you may have.

Intercession

If we trust in You, the Lord our God, we will be established; if we believe in Your prophets we will prosper. (2 Chronicles 20:20)

Take a few moments to intercede on behalf of your local, state or provincial, and national governments. Pray for spiritual revival in the nation and offer prayers regarding current events and concerns.

Affirmation

O Son of Man, You are going to come in the glory of Your Father with Your angels, and then You will reward people according to their works. (Matthew 16:27)

If anyone is ashamed of You and Your words in this adulterous and sinful generation, then You, the Son of Man, will be ashamed of that person when You come in the glory of Your Father with the holy angels. (Mark 8:38; Luke 9:26)

Blessed are the dead who die in You, Lord, from now on. They will rest from their labor, for their works will follow them. (Revelation 14:13)

Pause to reflect on these Biblical affirmations.

Thanksgiving

I was washed, I was sanctified, I was justified in Your name, Lord Jesus Christ, and by Your Spirit. (1 Corinthians 6:11)

Thanks be to God, the One who gives us the victory through You, our Lord Jesus Christ. Therefore let us be steadfast, immovable, abounding in Your work, knowing that our labor in You is not in vain. (1 Corinthians 15:57–58)

Pause to offer your own expressions of thanksgiving.

Closing Prayer

O God, You are the One who said, "Let light shine out of darkness"; and You made Your light shine in my heart to give me the light of the knowledge of Your glory in the face of Christ. But I have this treasure in an earthen vessel to show that this all-surpassing power is from You and not from me. (2 Corinthians 4:6–7)

Your grace is sufficient for me, for Your power is made perfect in weakness. Therefore, I will boast all the more gladly in my weaknesses, that the power of Christ may rest upon me. Therefore I can be content in weaknesses, in insults, in hardships, in persecutions and in difficulties for Christ's sake. For when I am weak, then I am strong. (2 Corinthians 12:9–10)

DAY 14

Adoration

> Your lovingkindness, O Lord, reaches to the heavens,
> Your faithfulness to the skies.
> Your righteousness is like Your mighty mountains;
> Your judgments are like the great deep.
> O Lord, You preserve people and beasts.
> How priceless is Your lovingkindness, O God!
> Your children find refuge in the shadow of Your wings.
> For with You is the fountain of life;
> In Your light we see light. (Psalm 36:5–7, 9)

> I will praise Your name in song, O God,
> And magnify You with thanksgiving. (Psalm 69:30)

Pause to express your thoughts of praise and worship.

Confession

> All Your paths are mercy and truth, O Lord,
> For those who keep Your covenant and Your
>   testimonies.
> For Your name's sake, O Lord,
> Pardon my iniquity, for it is great. (Psalm 25:10–11)

Ask the Spirit to search your heart and reveal any areas of unconfessed sin. Acknowledge these to the Lord and thank Him for His forgiveness.

Renewal

My struggle is not against flesh and blood, but against the rulers, against the authorities, against the powers of this dark world and against the spiritual forces of evil in the heavenly realms. Therefore, I will put on Your full armor, O God, so that I may be able to resist in the day of evil, and having done all, to stand. (Ephesians 6:12–13)

Since I have been raised with You, O Christ, I should seek the things above, where You are seated at the right hand of God. May I set my mind on the things above, not on the things on the earth, for I died, and my life is now hidden with You in God. When You, who are my life, appear, then I also will appear with You in glory. (Colossians 3:1–4)

Pause to add your own prayers for personal renewal.

Petition

In my distress may I seek Your favor, O Lord my God, and humble myself greatly before You, the God of my fathers, for I know that You are God. (2 Chronicles 33:12–13)

Pause here to offer prayers of petition regarding your family and your ministry. Ask for His help and guidance in sharing Jesus with others and helping others grow in Him. Ask for guidance in your vocation and your avocations. Offer prayers of petition regarding your activities for this day and any special concerns you may have.

Intercession

As the Father has sent You, You also send us, Lord Jesus. (John 20:21)

Take a few moments to intercede on behalf of local, national and world missions. Pray that the Great Commission would be fulfilled and for any special concerns you may have for missions.

Affirmation

In their hearts people plan their ways,
But You, Lord, determine their steps. (Proverbs 16:9)

Many are the plans in people's hearts,
But it is Your counsel, Lord, that will stand.
   (Proverbs 19:21)

There is no wisdom or understanding
Or counsel that can succeed against You, Lord.
   (Proverbs 21:30)

The word that goes forth from Your mouth
Will not return to You empty
But will accomplish what You desire
And achieve the purpose for which You sent it.
   (Isaiah 55:11)

Pause to reflect on these Biblical affirmations.

Thanksgiving

Father, You are the One who makes me stand firm in Christ
and You anointed me. You also sealed me and gave me Your
Spirit in my heart as a deposit. (2 Corinthians 1:21–22)

Thanks be to You, Father, for You always lead us in triumph
in Christ; and through us You spread everywhere the fragrance of the knowledge of Him. (2 Corinthians 2:14)

Pause to offer your own expressions of thanksgiving.

Closing Prayer

Through the law I died to the law so that I might live for
God. I have been crucified with You, O Christ, and it is no
longer I who live, but You live in me. The life that I now live
in the flesh, I live by faith in You, who loved me and gave
Yourself for me. (Galatians 2:19–20)

To me, to live in You, O Christ, means everything and to
die is gain. (Philippians 1:21)

DAY 15

Adoration

You, O Lord, are upright;
You are my Rock, and there is no unrighteousness in
  You. (Psalm 92:15)

I will seek You, Lord, and Your strength;
I will seek Your face continually.
I will remember the wonders You have done,
Your miracles, and the judgments of Your mouth.
  (Psalm 105:4–5)

Pause to express your thoughts of praise and worship.

Confession

If I am proud, I will be destroyed;
If I have a haughty spirit, I will fall. (Proverbs 16:18)

*Ask the Spirit to search your heart and reveal any areas of
unconfessed sin. Acknowledge these to the Lord and thank Him
for His forgiveness.*

Renewal

Lord, we learn from Your Word that when Uzziah became
strong, his heart became proud and he acted corruptly, and
he transgressed against You, the Lord God, and he entered
Your temple to burn incense on the altar of incense.
(2 Chronicles 26:16)

When I am blessed with abundance, may I beware lest my
heart become proud, so that I forget You, the Lord my God,
who provides all good things, and lest I think that it was my

power and the strength of my hand that brought this wealth. (Deuteronomy 8:12–14, 17)

Pause to add your own prayers for personal renewal.

Petition

> Answer me when I call to You, O my righteous God!
> You have relieved me from my distress;
> Be merciful to me and hear my prayer. (Psalm 4:1)

Pause here to petition God for growth in your character and personal discipline, and for physical health and strength. Ask that He empower you for spiritual warfare against the temptations of the world, the flesh and the devil. Offer prayers regarding your activities for this day and any special concerns you may have.

Intercession

May I help the weak and remember Your words, Lord Jesus, for You said, "It is more blessed to give than to receive." (Acts 20:35)

Take a few moments to intercede on behalf of the poor and hungry, the oppressed and persecuted, and those in control of world and national resources. Offer prayers for peace among nations and regarding current events and concerns.

Affirmation

> Your hands made me and fashioned me. (Psalm 119:73)

> Before You formed me in the womb, You knew me;
> Before I was born, You set me apart. (Jeremiah 1:5)

> You know me, O Lord;
> You see me and test my thoughts about You.
>   (Jeremiah 12:3)

Pause to reflect on these Biblical affirmations.

Thanksgiving

O God, You made Him who knew no sin to be sin for me, so that in Him I might receive His righteousness. (2 Corinthians 5:21)

You, O God, chose me in Christ, before the foundation of the world, to be holy and blameless in Your sight. In love You predestined me to be adopted as Your child through Jesus Christ, according to the good pleasure of Your will, to the praise of the glory of Your grace, which You bestowed upon me in the One You love. (Ephesians 1:4–6)

Pause to offer your own expressions of thanksgiving.

Closing Prayer

O Christ, You are the image of the invisible God, the first-born over all creation. For by You all things were created that are in heaven and on earth, visible and invisible, whether thrones or dominions or rulers or authorities; all things were created by You and for You. And You are before all things, and in You all things hold together. (Colossians 1:15–17)

O Lord my God, the heavens, even the highest heavens, the earth and everything in it belong to You. (Deuteronomy 10:14)

DAY 16

Adoration

O Lord of hosts, God of Israel, enthroned between the cherubim, You alone are God over all the kingdoms of the earth. You have made heaven and earth. (Isaiah 37:16)

> Mighty One, God, the Lord,
> You have spoken and summoned the earth
> From the rising of the sun to the place where it sets.
> (Psalm 50:1)

Pause to express your thoughts of praise and worship.

Confession

> There isn't anyone on earth who continually does good
> And never sins. (Ecclesiastes 7:20)

Ask the Spirit to search your heart and reveal any areas of unconfessed sin. Acknowledge these to the Lord and thank Him for His forgiveness.

Renewal

Whatever I do, whether in word or in deed, may I do all in Your name, Lord Jesus, giving thanks to God the Father through You. (Colossians 3:17)

May I abide in You, O Christ, so that when You appear, I will have confidence and not be ashamed before You at Your coming. (1 John 2:28)

Pause to add your own prayers for personal renewal.

Petition

> When I am afraid, I will trust in You,
> O God, whose word I praise.
> In You I have put my trust.
> I will not fear;
> What can mere mortals do to me? (Psalm 56:3–4)

Pause here to petition God for growth in your desire to know and please Jesus Christ. Pray for a greater love and commitment to Him, for the grace to practice His presence and for the grace to glorify Him in your life. Offer prayers regarding your activities for this day and any special concerns you may have.

Intercession

There is neither Jew nor Greek, there is neither slave nor free, there is neither male nor female, for we are all one in You, Christ Jesus. (Galatians 3:28)

Take a few moments to intercede on behalf of your local church, other churches, evangelism and discipleship ministries, educational ministries and any other special concerns you may have.

Affirmation

Those who love their father or mother more than You are not worthy of You; those who love their son or daughter more than You are not worthy of You. (Matthew 10:37)

Those who do not take up the cross and follow after You are not worthy of You. Those who find their life will lose it, and those who lose their life for Your sake will find it. (Matthew 10:38–39)

Pause to reflect on these Biblical affirmations.

Thanksgiving

O God, in Christ I have redemption through His blood, the forgiveness of sins, in accordance with the riches of Your grace, which You lavished on me with all wisdom and understanding. (Ephesians 1:7–8)

O God, You raised me up with Christ and seated me with You in the heavenly realms in Christ Jesus, in order that in the coming ages You might show the surpassing riches of Your grace in kindness toward me in Christ Jesus. (Ephesians 2:6–7)

Pause to offer your own expressions of thanksgiving.

Closing Prayer

The secret things belong to You, Lord God, but the things revealed belong to us and to our children forever, that we may observe Your words. (Deuteronomy 29:29)

Be exalted, O Lord, in Your strength;
We will sing and praise Your power. (Psalm 21:13)

DAY 17

Adoration

> Whoever is wise will consider Your lovingkindness,
>   O Lord. (Psalm 107:43)

> The sum of Your words is truth,
> And all of Your righteous judgments are eternal.
>   (Psalm 119:160)

You are the God of Abraham, the God of Isaac, and the God of Jacob. (Exodus 3:6)

Pause to express your thoughts of praise and worship.

Confession

> You have blotted out my transgressions like a thick
>   cloud
> And my sins like the morning mist.
> I will return to You, for You have redeemed me.
>   (Isaiah 44:22)

Ask the Spirit to search your heart and reveal any areas of unconfessed sin. Acknowledge these to the Lord and thank Him for His forgiveness.

Renewal

> Let me stop trusting in human beings, who only live for
>   a little while.
> For of what account are they? (Isaiah 2:22)

May I trust in You enough to honor You as holy in the sight of others. (Numbers 20:12)

Pause to add your own prayers for personal renewal.

Petition

Keep falsehood and lies far from me;
Give me neither poverty nor riches;
Give me only my daily bread,
Lest I be full and deny You and say, "Who is the Lord?"
Or lest I become poor and steal
And profane Your name, my God. (Proverbs 30:8–9)

Pause here to petition God for wisdom. Ask Him to develop your eternal perspective, to renew your mind with truth and to help you develop greater skill in each area of your life. Offer prayers regarding your activities for this day and any special concerns you may have.

Intercession

Father, this is my prayer for Your people: May their love abound more and more in full knowledge and depth of insight, so that they may be able to approve the things that are excellent, in order to be sincere and blameless until the day of Christ—having been filled with the fruit of righteousness that comes through Jesus Christ, to Your glory and praise. (Philippians 1:9–11)

Take a few moments to intercede on behalf of your immediate family and other relatives. Offer prayers for their spiritual, emotional and physical concerns.

Affirmation

Jesus preached the gospel of Your kingdom, O God, and said, "The time is fulfilled, and the kingdom of God is at hand. Repent and believe the good news." (Mark 1:14–15)

You have called me to go and proclaim Your kingdom. (Luke 9:60)

As I follow You, You will make me a fisher of men. (Matthew 4:19; Mark 1:17)

Pause to reflect on these Biblical affirmations.

Thanksgiving

I will not forget You, the God of my salvation;
I will remember the Rock of my refuge. (Isaiah 17:10)

O Lord, You are my God;
I will exalt You and praise Your name,
For You have done wonderful things,
Things planned long ago in perfect faithfulness.
    (Isaiah 25:1)

Pause to offer your own expressions of thanksgiving.

Closing Prayer

Great are You, Lord, and mighty in power;
Your understanding is infinite. (Psalm 147:5)

To fear You, Lord, is the beginning of wisdom;
All who practice Your commandments have good
    understanding.
Your praise endures forever. (Psalm 111:10)

DAY 18

Adoration

O Sovereign Lord, You are God! Your words are true, and You have promised good things to Your servant. (2 Samuel 7:28)

> I will sing of Your lovingkindness and justice;
> To You, O Lord, I will sing praises. (Psalm 101:1)

Pause to express your thoughts of praise and worship.

Confession

> The one You esteem is humble and contrite of spirit
> And trembles at Your word. (Isaiah 66:2)

Ask the Spirit to search your heart and reveal any areas of unconfessed sin. Acknowledge these to the Lord and thank Him for His forgiveness.

Renewal

May I love You, Lord my God, and serve You with all my heart and with all my soul. (Deuteronomy 11:13)

May I set my heart to honor Your name. (Malachi 2:2)

May I worship You, Lord my God, and serve You only. (Matthew 4:10)

Pause to add your own prayers for personal renewal.

Petition

May I take courage and not be afraid, for You, Lord Jesus, are with me. (Mark 6:50)

Pause here to petition God for spiritual insight so that you might have understanding of His Word. Ask for insight into your identity in Jesus Christ: that you might know who you are, what direction your life should take and what His purpose for your life is. Offer prayers regarding your activities for this day and any special concerns you may have.

Intercession

Those who love their brothers and sisters abide in the light, and there is no cause for stumbling in them. But those who hate their brothers and sisters are in the darkness and walk in the darkness and do not know where they are going, because the darkness has blinded their eyes. (1 John 2:10–11)

Take a few moments to intercede on behalf of other believers, such as your personal friends, those in ministry and those who are oppressed and in need.

Affirmation

Lord Jesus, with these words You teach us to be servants:

Disciples are not above their teacher, nor servants above their master. It is enough for disciples to be like their teacher, and servants to be like their master. (Matthew 10:24–25)

The greatest among us should be like the youngest, and the one who rules like the one who serves. For who is greater, the one who is at the table or the one who serves? Is it not the one who is at the table? But You, Jesus, came among us as the One who serves. (Luke 22:26–27)

Those who want to be first must be last of all and the servants of all. (Mark 9:35)

Pause to reflect on these Biblical affirmations.

Thanksgiving

You raised up Pharaoh for this purpose, that You might show him Your power and that Your name might be proclaimed through all the earth. (Exodus 9:16)

Others may intend evil, but You can use it for good to accomplish Your loving purposes. (Genesis 50:20)

Pause to offer your own expressions of thanksgiving.

Closing Prayer

> There is none like You, O Lord;
> You are great, and Your name is mighty in power.
> Who should not revere You, O King of the nations?
> It is Your rightful due.
> For among all the wise people of the nations
> And in all their kingdoms,
> There is no one like You. (Jeremiah 10:6–7)

> Father in heaven,
> Hallowed be Your name.
> Your kingdom come;
> Your will be done
> On earth as it is in heaven. (Matthew 6:9–10)

DAY 19

Adoration

You, O Lord of hosts, are wonderful in counsel
 and great in wisdom. (Isaiah 28:29)

You are the Lord,
And there is no savior besides You.
From ancient days You are He,
And no one can deliver out of Your hand;
You act, and who can reverse it? (Isaiah 43:11, 13)

Pause to express your thoughts of praise and worship.

Confession

Lord Jesus, people despised and rejected You;
You were a man of sorrows, and acquainted with grief.
And like one from whom others hide their faces,
You were despised, and we did not esteem You.
Surely You have borne our infirmities
And carried our sorrows;
Yet we considered You stricken,
Smitten by God, and afflicted.
But You were pierced for our transgressions,
You were crushed for our iniquities;
The punishment that brought us peace was upon You,
And by Your wounds we are healed.
All of us like sheep have gone astray,
All of us have turned to our own way,
And the Lord has laid on You the iniquity of us all.
 (Isaiah 53:3–6)

*Ask the Spirit to search your heart and reveal any areas of
unconfessed sin. Acknowledge these to the Lord and thank Him
for His forgiveness.*

Renewal

May I not become weary in doing good, for at the proper time I will reap a harvest if I do not give up. (Galatians 6:9)

May I not grieve Your Holy Spirit, O God, who marked me with a seal for the day of redemption. (Ephesians 4:30)

May I work out my salvation with fear and trembling, for it is You, O God, who work in me to will and to act according to Your good purpose. (Philippians 2:12–13)

Pause to add your own prayers for personal renewal.

Petition

May I obey those who are in authority over me with fear and trembling and with sincerity of heart, as I would obey Christ, not with external service as one who wants to please people, but as a slave of Christ, doing Your will, O God, from my heart. With good will may I serve, as if I were serving You and not people, knowing that I will receive back from You whatever good I do. (Ephesians 6:5–8)

Pause here to petition God for growth in love and compassion toward others. Offer prayers for your loved ones, for those who do not know Jesus and for those in need. Offer prayers regarding your activities for this day and any special concerns you may have.

Intercession

Lord, make me increase and abound in my love for believers and for unbelievers. (1 Thessalonians 3:12)

Take a few moments to intercede on behalf of friends, relatives, neighbors and coworkers who do not yet know salvation in Jesus Christ.

Affirmation

Lord Jesus,

You are God's beloved Son, in whom He is well pleased. (Matthew 3:17; Mark 1:11; Luke 3:22)

You are the Christ, the Son of the living God. (Matthew 16:16)

You are the Christ, the Son of God, who came into the world. (John 11:27)

You are God's Son, whom He has chosen. (Luke 9:35)

Your Father loves You and has given all things into Your hand. (John 3:35)

Pause to reflect on these Biblical affirmations.

Thanksgiving

I will give thanks to You, Lord, for You are good;
Your love endures forever. (1 Chronicles 16:34)

In my distress I called to You, Lord,
And cried to You, my God, for help.
You heard my voice from Your temple,
And my cry came before You, into Your ears.
You brought me out into a broad place;
You rescued me because You delighted in me.
(Psalm 18:6, 19)

Pause to offer your own expressions of thanksgiving.

Closing Prayer

You, O Lord, have declared, "I know the plans I have for you, plans to prosper you and not to harm you, plans to give you a future and a hope." (Jeremiah 29:11)

You leave Your peace with me; You give Your peace to me.
You do not give to me as the world gives. I will not let my
heart be troubled nor let it be fearful. (John 14:27)

DAY 20

Adoration

> You are the Lord, my Redeemer,
> Who formed me in the womb.
> You have said,
> "I am the Lord, who made all things,
> Who alone stretched out the heavens,
> Who spread out the earth by Myself." (Isaiah 44:24)

> Blessing and glory and wisdom
> And thanksgiving and honor and power and strength
> Be to You, our God, for ever and ever. Amen.
>   (Revelation 7:12)

Pause to express your thoughts of praise and worship.

Confession

> All my ways are pure in my own eyes,
> But You, O Lord, weigh my motives. (Proverbs 16:2)

*Ask the Spirit to search your heart and reveal any areas of
unconfessed sin. Acknowledge these to the Lord and thank Him
for His forgiveness.*

Renewal

May I revere Your glorious and awesome name—Lord my
God. (Deuteronomy 28:58)

> May I serve You, Lord, with fear and rejoice with
>   trembling. (Psalm 2:11)

> May I give You my heart
> And may my eyes delight in Your ways. (Proverbs 23:26)

Pause to add your own prayers for personal renewal.

Petition

May I learn to be content in whatever circumstances I am. Whether I am in need or in abundance, whether I am filled or hungry, let me learn the secret of being content in any and every situation. I can do all things through You, the One who strengthens me. (Philippians 4:11–13)

Pause here to petition God to help you be a faithful steward of your time, talents, possessions and relationships. Offer prayers of petition regarding your activities for this day and any special concerns you may have.

Intercession

We have acted very wickedly toward You. We have not obeyed the commandments, statutes, and ordinances that You gave Your servant Moses. (Nehemiah 1:7)

Take a few moments to intercede on behalf of your local, state or provincial, and national governments. Pray for spiritual revival in the nation and offer prayers regarding current events and concerns.

Affirmation

O Christ, You were in the world, and the world was made through You, and the world did not know You. You came to Your own, but Your own did not receive You. (John 1:10–11)

O God, no one has ever seen You, but Your only begotten Son, who is in Your bosom, has made You known. (John 1:18)

Pause to reflect on these Biblical affirmations.

Thanksgiving

Your power, O God, toward those who believe, is according to the working of Your mighty strength, which You exerted in Christ when You raised Him from the dead and seated Him at Your right hand in the heavenly realms, far above all rule and authority, power and dominion, and every title that can be given, not only in the present age but also in the one to come. (Ephesians 1:19–21)

You, God, who are rich in mercy, because of Your great love for me, made me alive with Christ even when I was dead in transgressions; it is by grace I have been saved. (Ephesians 2:4–5)

Pause to offer your own expressions of thanksgiving.

Closing Prayer

Now to You, the One who is able to establish us by the gospel and the proclamation of Jesus Christ, according to the revelation of the mystery that was kept secret for long ages past, but now is manifested and made known through the Scriptures of the prophets by Your command, O eternal God, and has been made known so that all nations might believe and obey You—to You, the only wise God, through Jesus Christ, be the glory forever. Amen. (Romans 16:25–27)

Adoration

> I will express the memory of Your abundant goodness
> And joyfully sing of Your righteousness.
> O Lord, You are gracious and compassionate,
> Slow to anger and great in lovingkindness.
> You are good to all,
> And Your tender mercies are over all Your works.
>   (Psalm 145:7–9)

> My Redeemer, the Lord of hosts is Your name;
> You are the Holy One of Israel. (Isaiah 47:4)

Pause to express your thoughts of praise and worship.

Confession

> Out of the depths I call to You, O Lord.
> O Lord, hear my voice,
> And let Your ears be attentive
> To the voice of my supplications.
> If You should mark iniquities,
> O Lord, who could stand?
> But there is forgiveness with You;
> Therefore You are feared. (Psalm 130:1–4)

*Ask the Spirit to search your heart and reveal any areas of
unconfessed sin. Acknowledge these to the Lord and thank Him
for His forgiveness.*

Renewal

If I died with You, I believe that I will also live with You,
knowing that You, Jesus Christ, having been raised from the
dead, cannot die again; death no longer has dominion over
You. For the death that You died, You died to sin once for all;

but the life that You live, You live to God. In the same way, may I consider myself to be dead to sin, but alive to God in You. (Romans 6:8–11)

Having begun in Your Spirit, may I not seek to be perfected by the flesh. (Galatians 3:3)

Pause to add your own prayers for personal renewal.

Petition

May I not hate my brother or sister in my heart, but reprove my neighbors frankly and not incur sin because of them. (Leviticus 19:17)

May I not take vengeance or bear a grudge against others, but may I love my neighbor as myself. (Leviticus 19:18)

Pause here to offer prayers of petition regarding your family and your ministry. Ask for His help and guidance in sharing Jesus with others and helping others grow in Him. Ask for guidance in your vocation and your avocations. Offer prayers of petition regarding your activities for this day and any special concerns you may have.

Intercession

I pray that Your Word, O Lord, may spread rapidly and be glorified, and that Your people may be delivered from perverse and evil men, for not all have faith. (2 Thessalonians 3:1–2)

Take a few moments to intercede on behalf of local, national and world missions. Pray that the Great Commission would be fulfilled and for any special concerns you may have for missions.

Affirmation

If the many died by the trespass of one man, how much more did Your grace, O God, and the gift that came by the grace of the one Man, Jesus Christ, overflow to the many.

And Your gift is not like the result of the one man's sin, for the judgment followed one sin and brought condemnation, but the gift followed many trespasses and brought justification. (Romans 5:15–16)

The law was added that the transgression might increase. But where sin increased, grace abounded all the more, so that just as sin reigned in death, so also grace might reign through righteousness to bring eternal life through You, Jesus Christ our Lord. (Romans 5:20–21)

Pause to reflect on these Biblical affirmations.

Thanksgiving

Once I was alienated from You, O God, and was an enemy in my mind because of my evil works. But now You have reconciled me, by Christ's fleshly body through death, to present me holy and blameless in Your sight and free from reproach. (Colossians 1:21–22)

My citizenship is in heaven; from there I also eagerly await You, my Savior, Lord Jesus Christ. You will transform my lowly body and conform it to Your glorious body by the power that enables You to subject all things to Yourself. (Philippians 3:20–21)

Pause to offer your own expressions of thanksgiving.

Closing Prayer

Blessed are You, the God and Father of our Lord Jesus Christ, the Father of mercies and the God of all comfort. (2 Corinthians 1:3)

You are a God of hope; fill me with all joy and peace as I trust in You, so that I may overflow with hope by the power of Your Holy Spirit. (Romans 15:13)

DAY 22

Adoration

You are the Lord; You do not change. (Malachi 3:6)

O God, You are light; in You there is no darkness at all.
(1 John 1:5)

I fear You, O God, and give You glory, because the hour of
Your judgment has come. I worship You, the One who made
the heavens and the earth, the sea and the springs of water.
(Revelation 14:7)

Pause to express your thoughts of praise and worship.

Confession

My ears had heard of You
But now my eyes have seen You.
Therefore I despise myself
And repent in dust and ashes. (Job 42:5–6)

*Ask the Spirit to search your heart and reveal any areas of
unconfessed sin. Acknowledge these to the Lord and thank Him
for His forgiveness.*

Renewal

May I not let any corrupt word come out of my mouth, but
only what is helpful for building others up according to their
needs, that it may impart grace to those who hear. (Ephesians 4:29)

I have been born again, not of perishable seed, but of imperishable seed, through Your living and abiding word, O God.
Therefore, may I put away all malice and all guile and
hypocrisy and envy and all slander. (1 Peter 1:23; 2:1)

Since I have been approved by You, O God, to be entrusted with the gospel, let me speak not as one who wants to please people but instead so as to please You, the One who tests my heart. May I not seek glory from people. (1 Thessalonians 2:4, 6)

Pause to add your own prayers for personal renewal.

Petition

May I not follow the crowd in doing wrong. (Exodus 23:2)

May I not accept a bribe, for a bribe blinds those who see and perverts the words of the righteous. (Exodus 23:8)

Pause here to petition God for growth in your character and personal discipline, and for physical health and strength. Ask that He empower you for spiritual warfare against the temptations of the world, the flesh and the devil. Offer prayers regarding your activities for this day and any special concerns you may have.

Intercession

Salvation belongs to You, Lord.
May Your blessing be on Your people. (Psalm 3:8)

Take a few moments to intercede on behalf of the poor and hungry, the oppressed and persecuted, and those in control of world and national resources. Offer prayers for peace among nations and regarding current events and concerns.

Affirmation

O God, You set me apart from the time I was born and called me through Your grace. (Galatians 1:15)

I have believed in You, Lord Jesus, so that I will be saved— I and my household. (Acts 16:31)

I am joined to You, Jesus Christ; I am one with You in spirit. (1 Corinthians 6:17)

None of us lives to himself alone and none of us dies to himself alone. If we live, we live to You, Lord; and if we die, we die to You. So whether we live or die, we belong to You. (Romans 14:7–8)

Pause to reflect on these Biblical affirmations.

Thanksgiving

When I was dead in my trespasses and in the uncircumcision of my flesh, O God, You made me alive with Christ. You forgave me all my trespasses, having canceled the written code, with its regulations, that was against me and was contrary to me; You took it away, nailing it to the cross. And having disarmed the powers and authorities, You made a public spectacle of them, triumphing over them by the cross. (Colossians 2:13–15)

God did not appoint me to suffer wrath but to obtain salvation through You, my Lord Jesus Christ. You died for me, so that, whether I am awake or asleep, I may live together with You. (1 Thessalonians 5:9–10)

Pause to offer your own expressions of thanksgiving.

Closing Prayer

The grace of the Lord Jesus Christ, and Your love, God our Father, and the fellowship of the Holy Spirit are with us. (2 Corinthians 13:14)

> We bless You, O Lord, forever!
> Amen and Amen. (Psalm 89:52)

DAY 23

Adoration

O God, will You indeed dwell on earth? Heaven and the highest heaven cannot contain You. (1 Kings 8:27)

> Your voice, O God, thunders in marvelous ways;
> You do great things that we cannot comprehend.
> (Job 37:5)

Pause to express your thoughts of praise and worship.

Confession

> O Lord, do not rebuke me in Your anger
> Or chasten me in Your wrath.
> Be merciful to me, Lord, for I am weak;
> O Lord, heal me, for my bones are in distress.
> My soul also is greatly troubled.
> How long, O Lord, how long? (Psalm 6:1–3)

Ask the Spirit to search your heart and reveal any areas of unconfessed sin. Acknowledge these to the Lord and thank Him for His forgiveness.

Renewal

May I be self-controlled and alert; my adversary the devil prowls around like a roaring lion looking for someone to devour. But may I resist him, standing firm in the faith, knowing that my brothers and sisters throughout the world are undergoing the same kind of sufferings. (1 Peter 5:8–9)

I will stand firm. I will gird my waist with truth, put on the breastplate of righteousness, fit my feet with the readiness of the gospel of peace and take up the shield of faith with which I will be able to quench all the fiery darts of the evil one. I will take the helmet of salvation and the sword of the Spirit, which is Your word, O God. With all prayer and petition, I will pray always in the Spirit, and to this end I will be watchful with all perseverance and petition for all the saints. (Ephesians 6:14–18)

Pause to add your own prayers for personal renewal.

Petition

O Lord, that You would bless me and enlarge my territory! Let Your hand be with me and keep me from evil, so it may not grieve me. (1 Chronicles 4:10)

Pause here to petition God for growth in your desire to know and please Jesus Christ. Pray for a greater love and commitment to Him, for the grace to practice His presence and for the grace to glorify Him in your life. Offer prayers regarding your activities for this day and any special concerns you may have.

Intercession

Lord Jesus, grace has been given to each one of us according to the measure of Your gift. And You gave some to be apostles, some to be prophets, some to be evangelists and some to be pastors and teachers, to equip the saints for the work of ministry so that Your body will be built up, O Christ. (Ephesians 4:7, 11–12)

Take a few moments to intercede on behalf of your local church, other churches, evangelism and discipleship ministries, educational ministries and any other special concerns you may have.

Affirmation

As Moses lifted up the snake in the desert, so You, Son of Man, had to be lifted up so that everyone who believes in You may have eternal life. (John 3:14–15)

Those who believe in You, Jesus, are not condemned, but those who do not believe are condemned already, because they have not believed in Your name—You who are the only begotten Son of God. (John 3:18)

Pause to reflect on these Biblical affirmations.

Thanksgiving

We are not to be ignorant about those who fall asleep or grieve like other people who have no hope. For if we believe that You, Jesus, died and rose again, even so the Father will bring with You those who have fallen asleep in You. According to Your own word, we who are alive and remain until Your coming will not precede those who have fallen asleep. For You Yourself will come down from heaven with a loud command, with the voice of the archangel, and with the trumpet of God, and the dead in You will rise first. Then we who are alive and remain will be caught up together with them in the clouds to meet You in the air. And so we will be with You forever. (1 Thessalonians 4:13–17)

Pause to offer your own expressions of thanksgiving.

Closing Prayer

> You are my hiding place;
> You will preserve me from trouble
> And surround me with songs of deliverance.
>   (Psalm 32:7)

> You will instruct me and teach me in the way I should go;
> You will counsel me and watch over me. (Psalm 32:8)

DAY 24

Adoration

> I praise You, Lord!
> My soul praises You!
> I will praise You while I live;
> I will sing praises to You while I have my being.
>   (Psalm 146:1–2)
>
> My mouth will speak Your praise, O Lord,
> And all flesh will bless Your holy name for ever and
>   ever. (Psalm 145:21)

Pause to express your thoughts of praise and worship.

Confession

O my God, I am too ashamed and disgraced to lift up my face to You, my God, because our sins have risen higher than our heads and our guilt has reached to the heavens. (Ezra 9:6)

Ask the Spirit to search your heart and reveal any areas of unconfessed sin. Acknowledge these to the Lord and thank Him for His forgiveness.

Renewal

May my attitude be the same as Yours, Christ Jesus; though You were in Your very nature God, You did not consider equality with Him something to be grasped, but emptied Yourself, becoming like a servant and being made in human form. And appearing as a human being, You humbled Yourself and became obedient to death, even death on a cross. (Philippians 2:5–8)

May I seek Your interests, Christ Jesus, rather than my own. (Philippians 2:21)

Pause to add your own prayers for personal renewal.

Petition

May I be strong and not lose courage, for my work will be rewarded. (2 Chronicles 15:7)

Pause here to petition God for wisdom. Ask Him to develop your eternal perspective, to renew your mind with truth and to help you develop greater skill in each area of your life. Offer prayers regarding your activities for this day and any special concerns you may have.

Intercession

May we encourage one another daily, as long as it is still called "Today," lest any of us be hardened by the deceitfulness of sin. (Hebrews 3:13)

Take a few moments to intercede on behalf of your immediate family and other relatives. Offer prayers for their spiritual, emotional and physical concerns.

Affirmation

Christ, You have completed the law so that there may be righteousness to everyone who believes. (Romans 10:4)

Faith comes from hearing, and hearing by Your word, Jesus Christ. (Romans 10:17)

My faith does not rest on human wisdom, but on Your power, O God. (1 Corinthians 2:5)

Pause to reflect on these Biblical affirmations.

Thanksgiving

It is a trustworthy saying that deserves full acceptance—You, Christ Jesus, came into the world to save sinners. I obtained mercy as the worst of sinners, so that You might display Your unlimited patience as an example for those who would believe in You for eternal life. (1 Timothy 1:15–16)

O God, You have saved me and called me with a holy calling, not according to my works but according to Your own purpose and grace. (2 Timothy 1:9)

Pause to offer your own expressions of thanksgiving.

Closing Prayer

There is now no condemnation for those who are in You, Christ Jesus, because the law of the Spirit of life in You has set us free from the law of sin and death. (Romans 8:1–2)

O God, in Christ we have obtained an inheritance, having been predestined according to Your plan as You work all things according to the counsel of Your will, that we who have trusted in Christ might be to the praise of His glory. (Ephesians 1:11–12)

Adoration

> To You, O God, belong wisdom and power;
> Counsel and understanding are Yours. (Job 12:13)

> You are holy;
> You are enthroned on the praise of Israel. (Psalm 22:3)

Pause to express your thoughts of praise and worship.

Confession

> What are people that You should magnify them,
> That You should set Your heart on them,
> That You examine them every morning
> And test them every moment? (Job 7:17–18)

Ask the Spirit to search your heart and reveal any areas of unconfessed sin. Acknowledge these to the Lord and thank Him for His forgiveness.

Renewal

May I flee youthful lusts and pursue righteousness, faith, love and peace with those who call on You out of a pure heart. (2 Timothy 2:22)

May I avoid foolish and ignorant disputes, knowing that they produce quarrels. As Your servant, O Lord, I must not quarrel, but be gentle toward all, able to teach and patient. (2 Timothy 2:23–24)

Pause to add your own prayers for personal renewal.

Petition

It is Your will, O God, that I be sanctified, that I abstain from immorality and learn to be in control of my own body in holiness and honor. For You did not call me to be impure, but to live a holy life. (1 Thessalonians 4:3–4, 7)

Pause here to petition God for spiritual insight so that you might have understanding of His Word. Ask for insight into your identity in Jesus Christ: that you might know who you are, what direction your life should take and what His purpose for your life is. Offer prayers regarding your activities for this day and any special concerns you may have.

Intercession

May I owe nothing to anyone except to love them, for those who love their neighbor have fulfilled the law. For the commandments, "You shall not commit adultery," "You shall not murder," "You shall not steal," "You shall not covet," and any other commandments there may be are summed up in this saying: "You shall love your neighbor as yourself." Love does no harm to a neighbor; therefore love is the fulfillment of the law. (Romans 13:8–10)

Take a few moments to intercede on behalf of other believers, such as your personal friends, those in ministry and those who are oppressed and in need.

Affirmation

In You, O Christ, are hidden all the treasures of wisdom and knowledge. (Colossians 2:3)

In You, O Christ, all the fullness of the Godhead lives in bodily form. (Colossians 2:9)

I have set my hope on You, the living God, who is the Savior of all people, especially of those who believe. (1 Timothy 4:10)

Pause to reflect on these Biblical affirmations.

Thanksgiving

God, Your grace was given to us in Christ Jesus before the beginning of time and has now been revealed through the appearing of our Savior, Christ Jesus, who abolished death and brought life and immortality to light through the gospel. (2 Timothy 1:9–10)

Your grace, my Lord, was poured out on me abundantly, along with the faith and love that are in Christ Jesus. (1 Timothy 1:14)

Pause to offer your own expressions of thanksgiving.

Closing Prayer

> I have seen You in the sanctuary
> And beheld Your power and Your glory.
> Because Your lovingkindness is better than life,
> My lips will praise You.
> So I will bless You as long as I live;
> I will lift up my hands in Your name.
> My soul will be satisfied as with the richest of foods,
> And my mouth will praise You with joyful lips.
>   (Psalm 63:2–5)

O God, You are able to do immeasurably more than all that we ask or think, according to Your power that is at work within us. To You be glory, in the church and in Christ Jesus throughout all generations, for ever and ever. (Ephesians 3:20–21)

DAY 26

Adoration

You, O Lord, are a compassionate and gracious God,
Slow to anger and abounding in lovingkindness and
   truth. (Psalm 86:15)

My flesh trembles in fear of You;
I stand in awe of Your judgments. (Psalm 119:120)

Pause to express your thoughts of praise and worship.

Confession

You are good and upright, O Lord;
Therefore You instruct sinners in Your ways.
You guide the humble in what is right
And teach the humble Your way. (Psalm 25:8–9)

*Ask the Spirit to search your heart and reveal any areas of
unconfessed sin. Acknowledge these to the Lord and thank Him
for His forgiveness.*

Renewal

May I keep Your words
And store up Your commands within me.
May I keep Your commands and live,
And may Your law be the apple of my eye.
May I bind them on my fingers;
May I write them on the tablet of my heart.
May I say to wisdom, "You are my sister,"
And call understanding my kinsman. (Proverbs 7:1–4)

May I carefully observe all Your commands—to love You, the Lord my God, to walk in all Your ways and to hold fast to You. (Deuteronomy 11:22)

Pause to add your own prayers for personal renewal.

Petition

May I be an example for other believers in speech, in behavior, in love, in faith and in purity. (1 Timothy 4:12)

Pause here to petition God for growth in love and compassion toward others. Offer prayers for your loved ones, for those who do not know Jesus and for those in need. Offer prayers regarding your activities for this day and any special concerns you may have.

Intercession

May I have mercy on those who are doubting. (Jude 22)

Take a few moments to intercede on behalf of friends, relatives, neighbors and coworkers who do not yet know salvation in Jesus Christ.

Affirmation

Jesus Christ, during the days You lived on earth, You offered up prayers and petitions with loud cries and tears to the One who could save You from death, and You were heard because of Your reverent submission. Although You were a Son, You learned obedience by the things You suffered; and being perfected, You became the source of eternal salvation for all who obey You, being designated by God as a high priest according to the order of Melchizedek. (Hebrews 5:7–10)

When You, O Christ, came as high priest of the good things that have come, You went through a greater and more perfect tabernacle—one not made with hands, that is to say, not a part of this creation. You did not enter through the blood of goats and calves; but through Your own blood, You entered the Most Holy Place once for all, having obtained eternal redemption. (Hebrews 9:11–12)

Pause to reflect on these Biblical affirmations.

Thanksgiving

We are looking for Your blessed hope and Your glorious appearing, Christ Jesus, our great God and Savior; You gave Yourself for us to redeem us from all iniquity and to purify for Yourself a people for Your own possession, a people zealous for good works. (Titus 2:13–14)

You, O Lord, will deliver me from every evil work and will bring me safely to Your heavenly kingdom. To You be glory for ever and ever. (2 Timothy 4:18)

Pause to offer your own expressions of thanksgiving.

Closing Prayer

O God, You comfort us in all our afflictions, so that we can comfort those in any affliction with the comfort we ourselves have received from You. (2 Corinthians 1:4)

> Satisfy us in the morning with Your loyal love, O Lord,
> That we may sing for joy and be glad all our days.
> (Psalm 90:14)

Adoration

> You are righteous in all Your ways
> And gracious in all Your works. (Psalm 145:17)

> You declare the end from the beginning,
> And from ancient times, what is still to come,
> Saying, "My purpose will stand,
> And I will do all My pleasure." (Isaiah 46:10)

Pause to express your thoughts of praise and worship.

Confession

I have sinned greatly in what I have done. But now, O Lord, take away the iniquity of Your servant, for I have acted very foolishly. (2 Samuel 24:10)

Ask the Spirit to search your heart and reveal any areas of unconfessed sin. Acknowledge these to the Lord and thank Him for His forgiveness.

Renewal

> May I return to You, my God,
> Maintain mercy and justice,
> And wait on You continually. (Hosea 12:6)

May I not live on bread alone, but on every word that comes from Your mouth, O God. (Matthew 4:4)

Pause to add your own prayers for personal renewal.

Petition

May I be above reproach and blameless as Your steward, O God—not self-willed, not quick-tempered, not given to wine, not violent, not fond of dishonest gain, but hospitable, a lover of what is good, sensible, just, holy and self-controlled. (Titus 1:6–8)

Pause here to petition God to help you be a faithful steward of your time, talents, possessions and relationships. Offer prayers of petition regarding your activities for this day and any special concerns you may have.

Intercession

When the children of Judah were victorious, it was because they relied on You, the God of their fathers. (2 Chronicles 13:18)

Take a few moments to intercede on behalf of your local, state or provincial, and national governments. Pray for spiritual revival in the nation and offer prayers regarding current events and concerns.

Affirmation

O God, to do Your work I must believe in Christ Jesus whom You have sent. (John 6:28–29)

This is Your commandment, Father: that we believe in the name of Your Son, Jesus Christ, and love one another as He commanded us. (1 John 3:23)

Father, You have sent Your Son to be the Savior of the world. If we confess that Jesus is Your Son, You abide in us and we abide in You. (1 John 4:14–15)

Pause to reflect on these Biblical affirmations.

Thanksgiving

When Your kindness and love appeared, O God my Savior, You saved me, not by works of righteousness that I had done, but according to Your mercy. You saved me through the washing of regeneration and renewal by Your Holy Spirit, whom You poured out on me abundantly through Jesus Christ my Savior, so that having been justified by Your grace, I might become an heir, having the hope of eternal life. (Titus 3:4–7)

My hope in You, Father God, is an anchor for my soul, both sure and steadfast, and it enters the inner sanctuary behind the veil, where Jesus the forerunner has entered on my behalf, having become a high priest forever, according to the order of Melchizedek. (Hebrews 6:19–20)

Pause to offer your own expressions of thanksgiving.

Closing Prayer

Father, You have qualified me to share in the inheritance of the saints in the light. For You have rescued me from the dominion of darkness and brought me into the kingdom of Your beloved Son, in whom I have redemption, the forgiveness of sins. (Colossians 1:12–14)

I make it my ambition to please You, Lord Jesus Christ, whether I am at home in the body or away from it. For we must all appear before Your judgment seat, that each one of us may receive what is due for the things we have done while in the body, whether good or bad. (2 Corinthians 5:9–10)

DAY 28

Adoration

O Lord, our Lord, we join Your heavenly host in praising You:

And the four living creatures, each having six wings, were full of eyes around and within; and they do not rest day or night, saying,

> "Holy, holy, holy is the Lord God Almighty,
> Who was, and is, and is to come." (Revelation 4:8)

Then a voice came from the throne, saying: "Praise our God, all you his servants, you who fear Him, both small and great!" (Revelation 19:5)

Pause to express your thoughts of praise and worship.

Confession

Truly I have sinned against You, the Lord, the God of Israel. (Joshua 7:20)

Ask the Spirit to search your heart and reveal any areas of unconfessed sin. Acknowledge these to the Lord and thank Him for His forgiveness.

Renewal

May I love my enemies and pray for those who persecute me. (Matthew 5:44)

Whatever I want others to do to me, may I also do to them, for this sums up the Law and the Prophets. (Matthew 7:12)

Pause to add your own prayers for personal renewal.

Petition

Since I have in You a great high priest who has passed through the heavens, O Jesus, I will hold firmly to the faith I confess. For in You I do not have a high priest who is unable to sympathize with my weaknesses, but one who has been tempted in every way, just as I am, yet one who is without sin. Therefore, I will approach the throne of grace with confidence, so that I may receive mercy and find grace to help me in my time of need. (Hebrews 4:14–16)

Pause here to offer prayers of petition regarding your family and your ministry. Ask for His help and guidance in sharing Jesus with others and helping others grow in Him. Ask for guidance in your vocation and your avocations. Offer prayers of petition regarding your activities for this day and any special concerns you may have.

Intercession

May I not forget to do good and to share with others, for with such sacrifices You are well pleased. (Hebrews 13:16)

Take a few moments to intercede on behalf of local, national and world missions. Pray that the Great Commission would be fulfilled and for any special concerns you may have for missions.

Affirmation

Thank You, Lord Jesus, that You expressed Your willingness to die for us when You said, "My Father loves Me because I lay down My life that I may take it up again. No one takes it from Me, but I lay it down of My own accord. I have authority to lay it down and authority to take it up again. This command I received from My Father." (John 10:17–18)

Unless a grain of wheat falls to the ground and dies, it remains alone. But if it dies, it bears much fruit. Those who love their lives will lose them, and those who hate their lives in this world will keep them for eternal life. (John 12:24–25)

Pause to reflect on these Biblical affirmations.

Thanksgiving

I have been chosen according to Your foreknowledge, Father, through sanctification of Your Spirit, for obedience to Jesus Christ and sprinkling of His blood; grace and peace are mine in abundance. (1 Peter 1:2)

Through Jesus I will continually offer to You, O God, a sacrifice of praise, that is, the fruit of lips that give thanks to Your name. (Hebrews 13:15)

Pause to offer your own expressions of thanksgiving.

Closing Prayer

May our Lord Jesus Christ Himself and You, our Father, who have loved us and have given us eternal consolation and good hope by grace, comfort our hearts and strengthen us in every good work and word. (2 Thessalonians 2:16–17)

O God, You are the blessed and only Sovereign, the King of kings and Lord of lords, the One who alone has immortality and dwells in unapproachable light, whom no one has seen or can see. To You be honor and eternal dominion. (1 Timothy 6:15–16)

DAY 29

Adoration

You reign, O Lord; You are clothed with majesty;
You are robed in majesty and are armed with strength.
Indeed, the world is firmly established; it cannot be
 moved.
Your throne is established from of old;
You are from everlasting.
Your testimonies stand firm;
Holiness adorns Your house,
O Lord, forever. (Psalm 93:1–2, 5)

You sit enthroned above the circle of the earth, O God,
And its inhabitants are like grasshoppers.
You stretch out the heavens like a curtain
And spread them out like a tent to dwell in.
You reduce rulers to nothing
And make the judges of this world meaningless.
 (Isaiah 40:22–23)

Pause to express your thoughts of praise and worship.

Confession

Forgive me when I desert You, the Rock who begot me,
And forget You, the God who gave me birth.
 (Deuteronomy 32:18)

Ask the Spirit to search your heart and reveal any areas of unconfessed sin. Acknowledge these to the Lord and thank Him for His forgiveness.

Renewal

Lord, by Your grace I want to hear the words, "Well done, good and faithful servant; you have been faithful with a few things; I will put you in charge of many things. Enter into My joy." (Matthew 25:21)

May I not love praise from people more than praise from You, O God. (John 12:43)

I am Your servant, Lord; let Your will be done in me according to Your word. (Luke 1:38)

Pause to add your own prayers for personal renewal.

Petition

May I not throw away my confidence; it will be richly rewarded. Let me persevere so that when I have done Your will, O God, I will receive what You have promised. (Hebrews 10:35–36)

Pause here to petition God for growth in your character and personal discipline, and for physical health and strength. Ask that He empower you for spiritual warfare against the temptations of the world, the flesh and the devil. Offer prayers regarding your activities for this day and any special concerns you may have.

Intercession

Many are asking, "Who will show us any good?"
O Lord, lift up the light of Your countenance upon us.
   (Psalm 4:6)

Take a few moments to intercede on behalf of the poor and hungry, the oppressed and persecuted, and those in control of world and national resources. Offer prayers for peace among nations and regarding current events and concerns.

Affirmation

O God, You raised Jesus from the dead, freeing Him from the agony of death, because it was impossible for Him to be held by it. (Acts 2:24)

Just as You, Father, raise the dead and give them life, even so Your Son gives life to whom He wishes. (John 5:21)

O God, You give life to the dead and call into being things that do not exist. (Romans 4:17)

Anyone who believes in Your Son, O God, has everlasting life. (John 6:47)

O God, You raised Jesus Christ and will also raise me up through Your power. (1 Corinthians 6:14)

Pause to reflect on these Biblical affirmations.

Thanksgiving

Though I have not seen You, Jesus, I love You; and though I do not see You now, I believe in You; I rejoice with joy that is inexpressible and full of glory, for I am receiving the end of my faith, the salvation of my soul. (1 Peter 1:8–9)

Since I am receiving a kingdom that cannot be shaken, may I be thankful and so worship You acceptably with reverence and awe, for You are a consuming fire. (Hebrews 12:28–29)

Pause to offer your own expressions of thanksgiving.

Closing Prayer

I will ascribe to You, O Lord, glory and strength.
I will ascribe to You the glory due Your name
And worship You in the beauty of holiness.
    (Psalm 29:1–2)

To You—the King eternal, immortal, invisible, the only God—be honor and glory forever and ever. (1 Timothy 1:17)

DAY 30

Adoration

You are the only God, the Father, from whom all things came and for whom I live; and there is but one Lord Jesus Christ, through whom all things came and through whom I live. (1 Corinthians 8:6)

Jesus, You are the radiance of God's glory and the exact representation of His being, upholding all things by Your powerful word. After You cleansed our sins, You sat down at the right hand of the Majesty on high, having become as much superior to angels as the name You have inherited is more excellent than theirs. (Hebrews 1:3–4)

Pause to express your thoughts of praise and worship.

Confession

You, Lord, do not see as people see. People look at my outward appearance, but You look at my heart. (1 Samuel 16:7)

Ask the Spirit to search your heart and reveal any areas of unconfessed sin. Acknowledge these to the Lord and thank Him for His forgiveness.

Renewal

May I be faithful, not doubting Your promises, O God, and not double-minded and unstable in all my ways. (James 1:6, 8)

May my walk be worthy of You, O God, who call me into Your kingdom and glory. (1 Thessalonians 2:12)

If I live according to the flesh, I will die; but if by Your Spirit I put to death the deeds of the body, I will live. For those who are led by Your Spirit are Your children. (Romans 8:13–14)

Pause to add your own prayers for personal renewal.

Petition

Since I have a great cloud of witnesses surrounding me, may I lay aside every impediment and the sin that so easily entangles, and run with endurance the race that is set before me, fixing my eyes on You, Jesus, the author and perfecter of my faith, who for the joy set before You endured the cross, despising the shame, and sat down at the right hand of the throne of God. May I consider You who endured such hostility from sinners, so that I will not grow weary and lose heart. (Hebrews 12:1–3)

Pause here to petition God for growth in your desire to know and please Jesus Christ. Pray for a greater love and commitment to Him, for the grace to practice His presence and for the grace to glorify Him in your life. Offer prayers regarding your activities for this day and any special concerns you may have.

Intercession

Just as the body is one, but has many parts, and all the parts of the body, being many, are one body; so also are You, O Christ. (1 Corinthians 12:12)

Take a few moments to intercede on behalf of your local church, other churches, evangelism and discipleship ministries, educational ministries and any other special concerns you may have.

Affirmation

Lord, You are my portion and my inheritance. (Numbers 18:20)

As for me and my household, we will serve You, Lord. (Joshua 24:15)

You will honor those who honor You, but those who despise You will be disdained. (1 Samuel 2:30)

Pause to reflect on these Biblical affirmations.

Thanksgiving

You did not redeem me from an aimless way of life, O Christ, with perishable things such as silver or gold, but with Your precious blood, as of a lamb without blemish or defect. (1 Peter 1:18–19)

How great is Your love, O Father, that You have lavished on me, that I should be called Your child—and I am! Therefore the world does not know me, because it did not know You. (1 John 3:1)

Pause to offer your own expressions of thanksgiving.

Closing Prayer

I am not ashamed, because I know whom I have believed and am convinced that You are able to guard what I have entrusted to You until that day. (2 Timothy 1:12)

May You, O God of peace—who through the blood of the eternal covenant brought back from the dead our Lord Jesus, that great Shepherd of the sheep—equip us in every good thing to do Your will, and may You work in us what is pleasing in Your sight, through Jesus Christ, to whom be glory forever and ever. (Hebrews 13:20–21)

DAY 31

Adoration

> You are He; You are the first,
> And You are the last. (Isaiah 48:12)

We confess that in the beginning was the Word, and the Word was with You, O God, and the Word was You. The Word was in the beginning with God. (John 1:1–2)

Lord Jesus, You are holy and true; You hold the key of David. What You open no one can shut, and what You shut no one can open. (Revelation 3:7)

Pause to express your thoughts of praise and worship.

Confession

Oh, my Lord, please do not hold against me the sin that I have foolishly committed. (Numbers 12:11)

Ask the Spirit to search your heart and reveal any areas of unconfessed sin. Acknowledge these to the Lord and thank Him for His forgiveness.

Renewal

> May I guard my heart with all diligence,
> For out of it flow the issues of life. (Proverbs 4:23)

May I not worry about tomorrow, for tomorrow will worry about itself. Each day has enough trouble of its own. (Matthew 6:34)

May I be ready, for You, O Son of Man, will come at an hour when I do not expect You. (Matthew 24:44; Luke 12:40)

Pause to add your own prayers for personal renewal.

Petition

May I not live the rest of my time on earth for my human desires, but for Your will, O God. For I have spent enough time in the past doing the will of those without You, when I walked in licentiousness, lusts, drunkenness, carousals, drinking parties and detestable idolatries. (1 Peter 4:2–3)

Pause here to petition God for wisdom. Ask Him to develop your eternal perspective, to renew your mind with truth and to help you develop greater skill in each area of your life. Offer prayers regarding your activities for this day and any special concerns you may have.

Intercession

My soul waits silently for You alone, O God,
For my hope comes from You.
You alone are my rock and my salvation;
You are my fortress, I will not be shaken.
In You are my salvation and my glory;
My rock of strength, my refuge is in You.
O, that others, too, will trust in You at all times
And pour out their hearts before You;
You are our refuge. (Psalm 62:5–8)

Take a few moments to intercede on behalf of your immediate family and other relatives. Offer prayers for their spiritual, emotional and physical concerns.

Affirmation

I have not yet come to the resting place and the inheritance that You, Lord my God, are giving me. (Deuteronomy 12:9)

You order my steps, O Lord,
And You will delight in my way;
Though I stumble, I will not be cast down,
For You uphold me with Your hand. (Psalm 37:23–24)

Lord, I have made You my refuge,
Even You, Most High, my habitation. (Psalm 91:9)

Pause to reflect on these Biblical affirmations.

Thanksgiving

You have given me life and shown me favor,
And Your care has preserved my spirit. (Job 10:12)

You are my shield, God Most High;
You save the upright in heart. (Psalm 7:10)

I will be glad and rejoice in Your love,
For You saw my affliction
And knew the anguish of my soul. (Psalm 31:7)

Pause to offer your own expressions of thanksgiving.

Closing Prayer

Blessed are You, the God and Father of our Lord Jesus Christ!
In Your great mercy You have given us new birth into a living hope through the resurrection of Jesus Christ from the
dead, and into an inheritance that is incorruptible, undefiled
and unfading, reserved in heaven for us. (1 Peter 1:3–4)

In Your great grace, O God, You called me to Your eternal
glory in Christ. After I have suffered a little while, You will
perfect, confirm, strengthen and establish me. To You be
the glory and dominion for ever and ever. Amen. (1 Peter
5:10–11)

PART THREE

Personal Prayer Pages

Prayer Concerns

Date: _____

_____

_____

Prayer Answered: _____

_____

Date: _____

_____

_____

Prayer Answered: _____

_____

Date: _____

_____

_____

Prayer Answered: _____

_____

Date: _____

_____

_____

Prayer Answered: _____

_____

Date: _____

_____

_____

Prayer Answered: _____

_____

Prayer Concerns

Date: _____

_____

_____

Prayer Answered: _____

_____

Date: _____

_____

_____

Prayer Answered: _____

_____

Date: _____

_____

_____

Prayer Answered: _____

_____

Date: _____

_____

_____

Prayer Answered: _____

_____

Date: _____

_____

_____

Prayer Answered: _____

_____

Prayer Concerns

Date: _____

_____

_____

Prayer Answered: _____

_____

Date: _____

_____

_____

Prayer Answered: _____

_____

Date: _____

_____

_____

Prayer Answered: _____

_____

Date: _____

_____

_____

Prayer Answered: _____

_____

Date: _____

_____

_____

Prayer Answered: _____

_____

Prayer Concerns

Date: _____

_____

_____

Prayer Answered: _____

_____

Date: _____

_____

_____

Prayer Answered: _____

_____

Date: _____

_____

_____

Prayer Answered: _____

_____

Date: _____

_____

_____

Prayer Answered: _____

_____

Date: _____

_____

_____

Prayer Answered: _____

_____

Prayer Concerns

Date: _____

_____

_____

Prayer Answered: _____

_____

Date: _____

_____

_____

Prayer Answered: _____

_____

Date: _____

_____

_____

Prayer Answered: _____

_____

Date: _____

_____

_____

Prayer Answered: _____

_____

Date: _____

_____

_____

Prayer Answered: _____

_____

Prayer Concerns

Date: _____

_____

_____

Prayer Answered: _____

_____

Date: _____

_____

_____

Prayer Answered: _____

_____

Date: _____

_____

_____

Prayer Answered: _____

_____

Date: _____

_____

_____

Prayer Answered: _____

_____

Date: _____

_____

_____

Prayer Answered: _____

_____

Prayer Concerns

Date: _____

_____

_____

Prayer Answered: _____

_____

Date: _____

_____

_____

Prayer Answered: _____

_____

Date: _____

_____

_____

Prayer Answered: _____

_____

Date: _____

_____

_____

Prayer Answered: _____

_____

Date: _____

_____

_____

Prayer Answered: _____

_____

Prayer Concerns

Date: _____

_____

_____

Prayer Answered: _____

_____

Date: _____

_____

_____

Prayer Answered: _____

_____

Date: _____

_____

_____

Prayer Answered: _____

_____

Date: _____

_____

_____

Prayer Answered: _____

_____

Date: _____

_____

_____

Prayer Answered: _____

_____

Prayer Concerns

Date: _____

_____

_____

Prayer Answered: _____

_____

Date: _____

_____

_____

Prayer Answered: _____

_____

Date: _____

_____

_____

Prayer Answered: _____

_____

Date: _____

_____

_____

Prayer Answered: _____

_____

Date: _____

_____

_____

Prayer Answered: _____

_____

Prayer Concerns

Date: _____

_____

_____

Prayer Answered: _____

_____

Date: _____

_____

_____

Prayer Answered: _____

_____

Date: _____

_____

_____

Prayer Answered: _____

_____

Date: _____

_____

_____

Prayer Answered: _____

_____

Date: _____

_____

_____

Prayer Answered: _____

_____

Prayer Concerns

Date: _____

_____

_____

Prayer Answered: _____

_____

Date: _____

_____

_____

Prayer Answered: _____

_____

Date: _____

_____

_____

Prayer Answered: _____

_____

Date: _____

_____

_____

Prayer Answered: _____

_____

Date: _____

_____

_____

Prayer Answered: _____

_____

Prayer Concerns

Date: _____

_____

_____

Prayer Answered: _____

_____

Date: _____

_____

_____

Prayer Answered: _____

_____

Date: _____

_____

_____

Prayer Answered: _____

_____

Date: _____

_____

_____

Prayer Answered: _____

_____

Date: _____

_____

_____

Prayer Answered: _____

_____